To My Valentine
With All My Love
Annie
2-14-24

SPIRITUAL HISTORY OF BRANSON
LAND OF THE OSAGE

SPIRITUAL HISTORY OF BRANSON

LAND OF THE OSAGE

by Gaye Newman Lisby

Branson, Missouri

ISBN: 978-1-257-03056-9

I owe a great debt to my consulting editor, Karen Pearson, for her hard work on this manuscript. I love her heart full of compassion for this land and this people. Special thanks also to Jan Johnson who has been eager to make this body of work available to this region.

**I appreciate the Nixa, MO. Fire Department for the use of the cover photo taken during a training fire several years ago. The photo is titled "Indian in the Fire." Can you see the warrior rising from the flames with club and hand upraised?*

For Steve, my loving patron and loving husband of nearly 30 years, and to my Ugi-ni-li, Colleen, a friend who "loveth at all times," and thinks what I write matters.

Cover Design by Jacob Lisby

Spiritual History Reader Endorsements

"My family has lived in the Ozarks from the beginning of its development, so I know the Ozarks and I know Gaye Lisby. In this book she has captured the heart of this area. With the historical facts and spiritual insight offered here, the reader will have a better understanding of why this region is spiritually significant." Pastor Tim Snider, Healing River Worship Center, Author of *Victorious Living-Becoming a Comeback Kid in a Knockdown World*

"Gaye Lisby has done extensive research for this book and has been able to effectively sort out facts from fiction. Her spiritual insight to the history of the Ozarks is enlightening and explains many of the struggles we currently face in maintaining a family friendly atmosphere in the region. Gaye is an excellent communicator and has presented the information in an interesting and readable manner." Herb Smith, Owner, KLFC Christian Radio, Branson, MO

"Gaye has done an exceptional job of compiling the spiritual history of this area in her book *The Spiritual History of Branson—Land of the Osage*. Through her discernment and insights, light is shed on some of the reasons for spiritual darkness that has overtaken the region. Because of her research, the reader is able to connect the dots of the spiritual issues that arise in this area. That gives great direction for knowing how to cover the land in prayer. Thank you, Gaye, for this insightful work." Jay and Kay Scribner, Gatekeepers Ministry, Branson, MO

"If you are interested in how you can pray and intercede for this region, this is a MUST READ book! Gaye Lisby, by the direction of the Holy Spirit, has been in a hearing and seeing position. She calls it research, we call it revelation—but whatever you call it, you must take advantage of this opportunity to get an overview of those things, (principalities and powers of wickedness) that plague our region." Pastors Aaron Glenn Artt and Sheliah Artt, CrossRoads International Revival Center, Branson, MO

"I have read Gaye Lisby's book and found it to be a powerful resource for those who are interested in history for the purpose of restoring the land through repentance and intercession. Gaye is an accurate researcher as well as a powerful intercessor. Her book will give you insight into the many layers of influence that have affected the land now known as Missouri. It certainly has my recommendation." Regina Shank, Missouri Apostolic Leader, United States Strategic Prayer Network

"In past seasons, the Church has received a great deal of understanding and knowledge that has done much to prepare us for God's purposes. But, there is a distinction in knowledge and revelation, with revelation being the key element in truly equipping the Body of Christ for these last days. Gaye Lisby's book brings forth to the Church both knowledge and revelation regarding this region and its people. Through Gaye's gifting for research and the prophetic, a valuable weapon has been handed to God's people. I pray we would be able to expose the enemy on this same lever throughout the regions of this nation. As well as being a great strategic resource, Gaye's book also challenges the Body of Christ to step up into her place of responsibility and accountability in these days of the Kingdom." Dr. Jay D. Morse, USSPN, Apostolic Coordinator for the State of Arkansas

CONTENTS

"Behold, I have put my words in your mouth. See I have this day set you over the nations and over the kingdoms, to root out and to pull down, to destroy and to throw down, to build and to plant" Jeremiah 1:9-10.

"Then the Lord said to me, "You have seen well, for I am ready to perform My word" Jeremiah 1:12.

Introduction

Since 1992 I have heard of perhaps thousands of people who have felt divinely directed to move to the Branson region. I have personally met hundreds of them. They are waiting. Waiting for what? Waiting for the fulfillment of a great move of God they believe God has appointed for these last days in this land among this people. Perhaps you are reading this book because you belong to this land and its people. Perhaps you are reading it because you are one of the thousands who were divinely directed to move here.

I did not have you in mind when I wrote the first edition of this book in 2004. I had only in mind to attempt to make sense of the strange and sometimes frightening things that had happened to me. I was minding my own business, owning my own business and raising my family. I never intended to have a confrontation with a witch. I never intended to become an intercessor or a spiritual history researcher. I never intended to receive profoundly disturbing prophetic dreams. I never intended to write this book.

However, since you are here and since there is a strong possibility you have this book because you are part of the divinely appointed, you might like to know where our land and our people came from. You might also like to know where we are going. This knowledge might help you find your place.

This is the story of my land and my people. If you stay and fight with us, perhaps they are yours too.

CHAPTER ONE

WORDS OF LIFE

"In the day that God is pouring out His Spirit, today, God is going to do a thing in this area where many streams are going to run together into one stream..." Reverend Tim Snider

For seven years I prayed and poured over thousands of pages of research material. From time to time, I would catch a glimpse of what intercessors call "the silver threads of redemption." These are words, phrases, and promises spoken through innocent lips, often created from unsuspecting minds, but always by the unction of the Holy Spirit. These words reveal our redemptive gifts and are signposts God has planted to help us find our way.

In addition, others would give me copies of prophetic words they had heard about our land and people. His destiny and design for our region began to be unfolded to many intercessors and confirmed by various prophetic voices. In this volume I have only included a few of those words, prophetic promises that I can personally verify were from reputable servants of the Lord. These give a vivid picture of what is in our Father's mind for this land.

Here are some examples of redemptive threads. In 1927 the Ozarks Playground Association developed a slogan for the Branson region:

Land of a Million Smiles

A 1935 edition of *The White River Leader* subtitled with this line:

Branson, MO. City of Bridges

Branson is named for Reuben Spalding Branson. The Branson Family heraldic crest states:

Dum Spiro Spero, Latin for *While I Breathe, I Hope*

Read the novel by Presbyterian minister and author Harold Bell Wright. The famous *Shepherd of the Hills* is replete with prophetic utterances as the old shepherd prepares a bride for her bridegroom. Read the poetry of native Ozarker Mary Elizabeth Mahnkey who loved this land and people and whose father was one of the original Bald Knobbers who immediately withdrew after the hanging of the Taylor Brothers. Listen to the native Ozarker's plaintive fiddle music. And, listen to the river. In prose, in verse, in song, and in creation, the sound of the Great Spirit of the Living God comes forth.

Consider this story recorded by Todd Parnell, a descendent of one of our early settlers in his book, *The Branson We Know, a Family Narrative.* His grandfather, B. A. Parnell, was a Branson businessman and later a banker, the mayor and a progressive civic leader during the Great Depression. B. A. Parnell remembered:

> Charlie Cobb from over near Forsyth told me about a pearl he had. Said one night he dreamed of the biggest pink pearl you've ever seen, deep in the White River, one half mile below Blackwell Ferry, just across the mouth of Cedar Creek. Charlie went out the next morning and dove down once, twice, and on the third time pulled up a big washboard mussel with that pearl in it, just like in his dream. He brought it to me. I wanted Opal to have it so I bought it from him.

How like Jesus to point us to the Pearl of Great Price found in the River of Life and use a humble Ozarker's life to highlight this message! He blessed this needy family with a jewel that sold for hundreds of dollars during the cash poor times of the early 1920s.

Consider these prophecies delivered by men and women inspired and controlled by the Great Spirit of the Living God:

There Is Going To Be an Awakening

Tim Snider

> "It's not going to be like before. It's not going to be like that which we have seen. But it's going to be a new thing. God is in this last day tired of divisions, tired of a spot here and a spot there. He's tired of a flame in this place and a flame in that place. He's tired of a color here and a color there. But in the day that God

is pouring out His Spirit, today, God is going to do a thing in this area where many streams are going to run together into one stream, the Word of Faith, the Power of God. Those little camps that have been this camp and that camp, this belief and that belief are going to begin to melt. God is going to sovereignly send the fire of God that is going to melt away the dross of our independence, going to melt away denominationalism, going to melt away the dross of our hatred and divisions.

And God is going to call His people up to a stream that is going to come into a river in one place. In this river God is going to demand that everybody lay down their differences and their little isms and schisms. God is going to speak to our hearts and everybody He brings into this place. And God is bringing into this place people that are going to be linked together and chained together. God is bringing into this area a people that will not be divided nor will be able to be torn apart, but a people that will be glued by the power of God's love and will work together in unity. They will have a different message. Many of them will teach a different part of the Word, but they will all benefit and flow together. They will lift each other up and not tear each other down.

God is going to take the competition of the church and He is going to rend it in two. He is going to tear it asunder because God is not into competition today. God is into unity and we will come together with gifts that God has given us. He's given us several gifts, but all are of the same spirit. He's given us gifts that will heal, gifts that will speak, gifts that will raise up, and gifts that will reveal. But God wants them all to work together in one place complementing each other, flowing together. Hallelujah! God is going to bring in ministries to this area that we never thought would be in this area. God is going to bring ministries here, and they will dwell here, and they will go in and out of this area and they will set up their place of residence here.

For God is calling into the middle of this country an area and a place where God is going to cause to flow forth into this country and into this world a people that are not ashamed of the gospel, a people that are not fighting with one another, but a people that are linked together and will say, "God is God. We are not here to represent ourselves, but we are here to represent God, the Lord God Jehovah." How dare anybody to rise up the flesh in the presence of the Lord!

The Holy Spirit is coming and going to strike down the egotism and the flesh. The ministries that He's called up, He's going to send in His hot flame and those that God gathers together in this area God is going to put the flame of His fire to them and melt them to the place they are willing to dwell one with another, to cooperate, to pray one with another, to say, "God we are only vessels, but you are God, Jesus you are Lord and the Holy Ghost is in charge." Hallelujah!

Many are being drawn here and saying "I don't know why." But God is bringing into this place, into this area people that have a hook in their jaw and are being brought together. God's going to put them together, those that formerly would not dwell together, those that before were competitive and would resist and repel each other. God is going to bring them together face to face and demand that they lay down their differences and demand that they become "nobodies" so that He can be the King of Kings and Lord of Lords. Hallelujah!

The churches in this area are going to have to come into the place where God has called us into. For everyone that will move in the move of God that God is bringing into this area, everyone will melt and everyone will come under the blood of Jesus or they will be without and shut out of the wall. Because God is not going to have those come in with divisive means and with self-motivation. God is going to cause them to be repelled and driven out, but it won't be by man but by the angels of God because God means in these last days for the church to become a body that has several parts, yet is joined together and dwells together; an arm working with a leg and the leg carrying forth that which it is supposed to carry, the body speaking, and the body moving and lifting up, the body working together in unity and power.

This will not be another Toronto nor will it be another Pensacola or anything that we have seen before for God is taking us from step to step from glory to glory and from faith to faith. It is time we say, "God, let it happen!" Hallelujah! It's a new day. It's a new Church.

God's going to bring everybody under one headship. And if they will not come under one headship, then God is going to chastise those that will not come under the headship of Jesus Christ. Denominations are going to begin to fade. The color is going to begin to blend. God is going to bring the color of different denominations. God is going to bring the gifts that He purposed in the beginning. In those places He's going to bring back alive the gifts that started in the beginning and they are going to come and dwell together. There are going to be those that come into this area that God uses mightily in miracles and wonders. There are going to be those that come into this area that can teach the Word of God in faith and that will cause even the most doubtful person to come alive and burn with the fire of the Word of God. God's going to bring people into this area that will be able to look out across the congregation and just with a look from their eyes people will fall on the floor and say, "God forgive me, I'm a sinner." God is going to bring people into this area that have great and powerful gifts, but none will be elevated, nor will anybody be king. There's only one king and that's Jesus Christ. He's Lord of all! He's Lord of all! Hallelujah!

We must get our eyes off of our preconceived ideas. We must forget our idols and our images. We must forget what we would like it to be and we must forget what our opinion is. For God is saying to us today, "I am God and I will surprise you and I will bring upon you that which you will look at and wonder and say, 'What is this thing for it's never been this way before.'" But God is going to come in His glory and His power and we will know His glory and we will know His voice. God will speak to us and we will say "Yes Lord." He will move and we will say, "God you are awesome." He will be glorified and none will dare to raise their head in the presence of the Lord.

The devil knows this is being brought together. The devil knows this is happening. He's sending in those that would come and bring division and those that would try to stop and those that would try to bring attention to themselves. But I want you to know that God in His sovereignty and in His power is saying to us today, "Keep your eyes on Me because they will fall short, they will fall short, they will fall short, but I will produce what I have called and what I have said, for my Word is carefully watched and I will perform that which I have spoken. And I will lift up who I will lift up and I will put down who I will put down. None shall reign unless I say. None shall move unless I speak. None shall be glorified for the glory of the Lord is going to captivate a nation."

But many are going to look back and stand back with enmity in their hearts and say, "I don't like it and it's not my way." And the fire of God will come upon our hearts and He will say, "My way or no way! My way, or no way!" The Baptists and the Pentecostals, the Catholics and the Charismatics, the Lutherans and the Methodists, the Independents and those that are renegades and don't want to be with anybody who want to start their own little groups and don't want to go together with anybody, God is going to come upon them and say, "Make a choice today! Either you will follow Me and put down your enmity and your divisions or I will remove my glory from you and make it obvious before men that my glory has departed, for my glory will no longer tolerate those things nor will I be patient with those that want to elevate the flesh, but my spirit will come upon them like a fire, like a burning brand that will cause the heart to melt before ME."

When we decide that God is going to be all, then that's when God is going to move. But God has already started a plan. He's already begun.

(This is not coming from my (prepared message) folks. This ignited in my spirit just a few minutes ago and I've spoken to you what God put into my heart. I've got a message, and boy it's a good one too. I wanted to preach but this is what we're doing now.)

God is calling to us and saying, "Will you accept me? Will you accept my move when it is not that which you desire? Will you accept my move when it doesn't include you, in lifting you up? Will you accept my move if it comes through someone else? Will you glorify God when you see the Spirit of the Lord moving in someone else? Or will you withdraw and say, “If it doesn't come through me and my church, I won't accept it.” God is speaking to us today and saying it's time to lie down, it's time to lie down and it's time to let God rise up. Hallelujah!

O, thank God there is a power of worship that is coming into this area like we've never known before! Hallelujah! Praise God! There is a power of worship that is going to fill this area like we've never known before. People are going to come and just be caught up in the worship of God. There are those who don't even believe in God, yet when they come and begin to experience the worship of God, they will be caught up and drawn in the worship of God. It will draw them like a mighty drawing. Hallelujah! O, thank God His glory is returning! His glory is coming in a people that will say, "God, it's yours, it's yours, it's yours." Hallelujah!

O Church, listen to me! We've got to become a people obedient. We've got to become a people willing and we've got to become a people of God with a fire in our hearts, without selfish ambition and motivation. We've got to be motivated by the heart of God. God is tired of the fleshly demonstrations of egotism. And His fire is going to melt the hearts of His people. It's already begun, but we've got to be to a place where we say, "Yes Lord, do it, yes Lord, do it."

I believe there's a Great Awakening coming to this area and it's not going to be like anything you've ever known. Toronto has been glorious. It's going to have an ingredient like Toronto, but it's not going to be Toronto. Pensacola has been glorious, but it's going to be different. It's not going to be like Pensacola, but it's going to have an ingredient of Pensacola. God is going to raise up something that we've never seen before. But all those that know God and all those that have a heart for God are going to recognize and they're going to hear and the minute they hear, I said, the minute that they hear their heart is going to leap within them and they're going to be drawn with a mighty drawing and they are going to begin to say, "This is it! This is it! This is God! Hallelujah!"

Praise God, there's going to be an awakening coming to this area that is not going to be the kind of healing revival like in Toronto. It's not going to be just the power of transformation and salvation like in Pensacola, but there is going to be another ingredient and it's going to be the awesome presence and glory of God that is going to come and touch bodies and people are going to be healed. People are going to realize the glory of the Lord and the power of God is going to be demonstrated like we've not seen before. God is speaking this: "If I can't find a people here, I will bring in and raise up a people. If I can't find a people who are here, I will bring in and raise up a people who will obey me and say, "Yes."

I don't know about you Church, but I don't want to be left out. I don't want to lead. I don't want to be the big shot because God's not going to have any big shots. I just want to be a part of it. I don't want to be the one on the outside standing back with my arms crossed and a spirit of criticism saying, "Well, it just ain't like I like it!" I'm going to be one of those right in the middle experiencing the glory of Almighty God! Hallelujah!"

An Outpouring Into The Tri-State Area

Jeanne Wilkerson

"There's going to be an outpouring into a Tri-State area: Missouri, Arkansas, and Kansas. This Tri-State area will be welded together. Look for the mighty deluge which is yet to fall on you. You (Missouri) are known as the "Show Me" state. Well, you're going to get it," saith the Spirit of the Lord. "Look for the work of the Tri-State area. The Spirit is saying, even Texas may come in on some of this. Texas is going to give you much support and Missouri and Arkansas and Kansas will be the beneficiaries. And, even as Oklahoma—that is like a great spiritual bank where I've invested much of the divine resources of God, and out of the great state is spreading out like radar fingers into the darkness of the night. Much is going out of that area of Oklahoma. I have set aside such an area for certain things. I'm going to be now calling it forth, for the time is at hand," saith the Spirit of the Lord."

Outpouring of Fire

Guy Johnston

"There is going to come a mighty revival, the likes of which has never been seen in this city. For even now, I see in my spirit, a great outpouring—an outpouring of Fire. The history books will record it. Many will come from far and from near to this place because of the outpouring of the Holy Ghost.

Many, many who have gone the way of the prodigal son shall return with joy in their hearts as a result of the outpouring of glory; and they shall be restored, and there shall be great joy in this city because of the outpouring.

Say not in your heart that it shall come in the future for it is even now that I have begun to pour out my Spirit. There shall be the watering, the planting, the watering, and there shall be the reaping. Some will plant more than others. Some will water more than others, but all shall be involved in the increase. And so it is even now that this body is in the planting process, and that which shall take place in this place shall be told around the world because of the mighty God who planned and purposed in His heart and His mind to do His good pleasure.

And yes, it shall shake up. I shall shake up. I shall shake up that which has been established by man for they have tried so hard to bring what I desired, but it has not been by My Spirit and My power. There shall a river flow of My Spirit into every denomination that exists among you. A river of My Spirit will visit them, yes; even you will be a part of it. Even you shall help. And many will have a choice to jump in. Many will have the choice to not go with the river.

If I were to tell you all that shall happen in your midst you would not believe it, says the Lord. It's much bigger than you think. It's greater impacting than what you think. I'm a big God – I do things in a big way. And I shall sweep every, every part of the earth. I shall sweep, and it's happening even now.

Many seek My great power. But I say it is My great love that I'm pouring out in this hour. Not in a shower, but an overflowing never ending outpouring of My Spirit. The latter rain and former rain together. The glory of the latter house shall be greater than that of the former.

(I see – I see- Oh – I see – I wish I could tell you what I see. Oh Jesus. I see multitudes coming to the hill of the Lord, and leaving the hill of the Lord changed. And going out to the uttermost part of the earth with Fire – the Fire of the Holy Ghost. And that hill, that hill of Zion; God is establishing in this city.)

Be not afraid to pray and to pay the price! Many souls, souls are weighed in the balance. Many of those who once had My touch await your touch. Look not on the outward of these for the garment of sin and the flesh are upon them. And remember that I am a God who does not look on the outward, but looks on the inward. I love these who have gone the way of the prodigal. I have not forgotten them. I have prayed for them that their faith would fail them not.

Judge not that you be not judged. Oh, ah, oh, oh, - Touch not Mine anointed; do My prophets no harm. Touch not My anointed, do My prophets no harm. Hear ye the words of the prophet – so shall ye prosper, so shall ye be established.

(I see - I see some that God has touched in different parts of the world: Evangelist, mighty men – mighty men of God, powerful men of God that will come in contact with this fellowship and be instrumental in this mighty revival that's coming. These are men who will shake the gates of hell when they come to a place. These are men who do not seek the applause of men. Prepare to receive them, prepare to receive them and criticize not that which you do not understand. Let love be the rule in your heart.)

Many have been sent to this place and throw up their hands and say, "Why?" They look around and say, "Why have I been sent here, or have I really been sent here?" The Lord would say: "It shall be seen. It shall be known. Oh, will it be known! It will be seen by each why they have been drawn here." Oh, and some that have left will come back."

Special Last Day Move

Clyde J. Avery

"Thus saith the Lord, do not let this slip from you. This nation will not be turned over to the devil. Start claiming this nation. I, the Lord God, doth move on the face of the earth. I, the Lord God, am moving by My Spirit across the land. As My great river that flows down near the center of the nation, bringing many streams together, so My river is flowing. Take note and hear what I, the Lord, have to say. In the State of Missouri I have twelve assemblies that I, the Lord, am burning a fire in. Lightning will flash out of Missouri. As My great river flows I will, saith the Lord, flow out of Missouri into many states. *I have chosen the center part of this nation to move out of.* This spiritual water shall flow out into many states that have their natural streams and rivers draining into My great river. I, the Lord, have a special last day move even now in 14 states. Even as false religion was seen in Missouri a few days ago, (the 1999 visit to St. Louis by the Pope) I will, saith the Lord, show forth My power. Thus, saith the Lord, out of the shadows I will raise up a leader that will lead this nation in righteousness. As my spiritual river flows out of Missouri, ask of Me for your state and county."

I Must Be Beckoned

Tim Snider

"Hear it! Listen, my people! Hear the rumble for as the storm fronts collide so my glory is spreading and colliding with the evil of the world. As those fronts hit, there's lightning, and thunder and wind that's contrary. There's force.

But as my glory is spreading across the land with a rumble of confrontation, with a rumble of war, with lightning and thundering of warfare, listen! For my glory moves, my presence moves. But I must be beckoned. I spoke to you promises and I spoke truths and declared to you the greatness of my intentions. But I must be beckoned to your area and to your region. I must be beckoned. You must desire my presence and my glory. I must be beckoned for the front will only move as the people beckon.

As my people beckon, there is no warfare that can defeat me. For as my people beckon, I move the line for the line is mine. If my people do not beckon, I cannot come.

Listen! Soon the line will be at your South East border! Will you beckon? Will you call to me? Will I be able to come and fulfill the intentions of my will? I must be beckoned!"

I think it is important to note that none of the speakers of the foregoing prophecies knew about the other's words. I collected these over the years of prayer and research as I met with intercessors. If you have heard the clarion call of the Holy

Spirit, you know that it is time to beckon the Lord to our region. He is more than ready.

The Truth About Corrie ten Boom

In the first edition of my book, I made what I found out later to be a troublesome error. For years I had heard about a prophecy that supposedly Corrie ten Boom gave concerning this region. In one version, supposedly Northwest Arkansas was especially mentioned. In another version, supposedly Branson was mentioned.

Yet another version had Corrie ten Boom as a speaker at School of the Ozarks (now College of the Ozarks) when she supposedly prophesied over the region. Long-time President of the college and personal family friend of mine, Dr. M. Graham Clark responded when I asked him about this, "Who is Corrie ten Boom?" He then proceeded to assure me she never visited the region.

Another version had co-founder of Silver Dollar City Jack Herschend flying with Corrie in a plane over the region when she prophesied. The Herschend's assured me this never took place.

Another version had Corrie ten Boom as the prophetic impetus for Gary Smalley's ministry move to the Branson region. However, in an article in *Branson Living*, a magazine which I published in the 1990s, Smalley talked about his kids attending Kanakuk Kamps during the summers. His trips here caused him to fall in love with the area. I spoke to Greg Smalley by phone and he said he remembered his father knowing Corrie and even having a small place for her to stay in Chicago when she passed through, but he knew nothing of a prophetic word from her concerning Branson.

Another version, and one which I erroneously printed in my first edition, had Corrie visiting Northwest

Arkansas, seeing angels and prophesying what they supposedly said. She supposedly appeared with Paul Crouch on TBN in 1980 and spoke that word. I am sad that I printed a copy of what appeared to be a newspaper clipping of the supposed event. I broke the cardinal rule of news reporting by propagating an unconfirmed report with no verifiable source.

Two years after the publication of my book, I received a letter via Diane Willits of Promise Keepers in Arkansas who had received it from Lisa Lyons of the Arkansas Concert of Prayer. The letter was from Pam Rosewell Moore. I later spoke to Pam personally and found her relieved to be able to, as she called it, "address this myth." Pam had served Corrie as personal companion and assistant from April 1, 1976 until Corrie's death on April 15, 1983. In the letter dated February 21, 2005 she wrote:

> To: My brothers and sisters in Northwest Arkansas
> Dear Friends,
>
> I have wanted to be in touch with you for several years and am so glad to have that opportunity now. In the twenty-two years since the death of Corrie ten Boom on her 91st birthday, April 15, 1983, countless inquiries have reached me by letter, telephone and e-mail concerning a prophecy she is alleged to have made regarding revival in Northwest Arkansas. These reports vary in their descriptions of where and how the alleged prophecy was given, but all focus on a claim of nationwide revival starting in Northwest Arkansas. I was Corrie ten Boom's personal assistant and constant companion from April 1, 1976 until her death on April 15, 1983. During this time I lived with Corrie permanently. Her home was my home for seven years, whether

it was a motel or somebody's house when we traveled, or her rented house in California in the last years of her life. I accompanied her on all trips and was present for interviews and functions where she was featured. I can confidently say that I know what she spoke publicly from the time I became her assistant until a stroke rendered her incapable of speaking. We also spoke privately about many things, including her ministry.

No such prophecy was made during my seven years with Corrie. We never visited Arkansas together nor did she talk to me about such a prophecy previously made either inside or outside of Arkansas during the time period of April 1, 1976 – August 23, 1978.

On August 23, 1978 Corrie suffered a serious stroke, one effect of which was that she lost her ability to speak. She was unable to travel or speak after that date, either publicly or to me privately. She died on April 15, 1983, without speaking again following her stroke. The overwhelming majority of the alleged prophecies include dates of the late 1970s and early 1980s. She did not speak during this time period. Corrie's previous companion, who was with her constantly for nearly nine years, has confirmed that no such prophecy was made between the years 1967-1976. Thorough attempts have been made to track down a purported video recording. There is no such video recording, nor film, nor audio recording.

My main purpose in writing to you is simply to present the facts, but I cannot resist, out of deep love and respect for Corrie ten Boom, the adding of a personal note. While I can certainly understand the deep longing and prayers of believers in Northwest Arkansas for true revival, I am mystified by this hankering after an unfounded rumor.

Only the Lord can bring revival. In responding to this kind of rumor about her when she was well, Corrie herself would write words such as: “Revival is the work of the Holy Spirit, not Corrie ten Boom.” The descriptions in the reports reaching me are completely against her character and behavior. I will be most grateful if you will assist me in the quashing of this false rumor. Thank you very much.

In God’s love,
Pam Rosewell Moore
Address: P.O. Box 2644, Waxahachie, TX 75168.E-mail: pam@moorelifelessons.net
Web site: www.moorelifelessons.net

To those who read my first edition, I owe a humble apology for lending credence to a myth. As you read the spiritual history of our land and our people keep in mind that many clear and respected prophetic voices have spoken concerning the Branson region and the move of God we are anticipating. However, let us take the good advice offered by our sister Pam Rosewell Moore and remember, “Revival is the work of the Holy Spirit, not Corrie ten Boom.”

The Third Great Awakening will not come to our land and people because we erroneously thought Corrie ten Boom said so. Jesus’ saving, healing, delivering power and glory will cover our land and our people because He wants to and because we fervently pray that He will.

As you discover your spiritual destiny here in the Branson region, perhaps it would help you to know what came before the prophecies. Perhaps it would also help you to know what has been opposing the anticipated move of God. Perhaps in knowing you will be able to more effectively bring your valuable part to this great work to which He has called us. If you are a native Ozarker, God bless you for your faithful prayers and devoted intercession. If you're a "come-here," may God also bless you! May you be strong and very courageous, and may the victory bring honor and glory to our Great King!

CHAPTER TWO

WHAT SINS ARE YOU TALKING ABOUT?

"If you know the enemy and you know yourself, you need not fear the result of one hundred battles. If you know yourself but know not the enemy, for every victory gained you will also suffer defeat. If you know neither the enemy nor yourself, you will succumb in every battle." Sun Tzu

This body of research is offered with three specific purposes in mind: repentance, strategy and harvest. First, we must know and understand the sins of our fathers in this region. This understanding will help us identify those same sins which may be prevalent in our generation so that repentance for them can be made. Remember the Word of the Lord, "If my people, which are called by my name, shall humble themselves, and pray, and seek my face, and turn from their wicked ways; then will I hear from heaven, and will forgive their sin, and will heal their land" (II Chronicles 7:14).

Second, understanding the movements of enemy spirits throughout the history of our region can help us identify their strategies and destroy their forces. Every good army works with good intelligence, information that helps place troops in the right place at the right time. Spiritual warfare is no different. Hosea wrote, "My people are destroyed for lack of knowledge: because thou hast rejected knowledge, I will also reject thee, that thou shalt be no priest to me: seeing thou hast forgotten the law of thy God, I also will forget thy children," (Hosea 4:6). We cannot afford to be ignorant of Satan's devices. Does this mean we need to infiltrate a cult in order to know how to dismantle it? Absolutely not! However, we do need to understand the elaborate deceptions and false mindsets that easily ensnare our people and are often issued forth from occult activity. Spiritual history research and spiritual mapping help to identify the methods the enemy has used against the people who live here.

The third reason for this book is to prepare the Church for the harvest. Bringing souls to the knowledge of our wonderful Savior is the main reason for any Great Awakening. Once the sins of our region have been acknowledged and brought before the Lord in humble repentance, and once enemy strategies are revealed and broken, the blind will suddenly see. We must be there with the Gospel of Jesus Christ so clearly preached in word and action so that every church and home becomes a maternity ward. These precious newborns will need to understand what ensnared them and then receive solid, biblical discipleship to keep them from falling.

If left to itself, history simply repeats itself. This research is offered with the hope we can break the cycle of sin and shame in our land among our people and set a new course, a glorious course, one that will honor our Royal Lord.

Show My People Their Transgression

The prophet Isaiah best articulates what I intend to do first. "Cry aloud, spare not, lift up thy voice like a trumpet, and show my people their transgression and the house of Jacob their sins," (Isaiah 58:1). But why research the sins of our fathers, the sins of generations long dead? Are we in modern times somehow responsible for the sinfulness of their lives? A resounding "yes" comes from God's own lips.

In Exodus 34:6-7, "The Lord passed before Moses and proclaimed, 'The Lord, the Lord, a God merciful and gracious, slow to anger, and abounding in steadfast love and faithfulness, keeping steadfast love for thousands, forgiving iniquity and transgression and sin, but who will by no means clear the guilty, visiting the iniquity of the fathers upon the children and the children's children to the third and fourth generation.'"

One may argue that this scripture pertains only to familial sins and not to sins of a city, a region, or a nation. Yet Ezekiel chapter 22 shows us a different picture. The prophet makes indictments against the city of Jerusalem for murders, making and worshipping idols, oppressing parents, oppressing those of a different race, vexing widows and orphans, despising God's holy things, profaning the Sabbath, carrying slanderous tales, committing lewdness, incest, homosexuality, adultery, murder for hire, charging interest for money lent (to their own people), greedily gaining by extortion, and forgetting God.

Notice in verses 25-29 on whom God issues judgments. Verse 25 judges the prophets, verse 26 judges the priests, verse 27 judges the civil rulers, and verse 29 judges the people. An intercessor was sought and sadly not found. In verse 31 judgments against the city were poured out.

Since the first edition of the book came out, some Believers have argued that we are not responsible for the sins of our forefathers. They point to Jeremiah 31:29, "In those days they shall say no more, 'The fathers have eaten a sour grape, and the children's teeth are set on edge.'" Clarke's Commentary on the Bible says that this is a proverbial expression for, "The children suffer for the offenses of their parents." This is explained in the next verse: "Every one shall die for his own iniquity." No child shall suffer Divine punishment for the sin of his father; only so far as he acts in the same way can he be said to bear the sins of his parents."

That, my brothers and sisters, is the rub. Sins become generational when no outside opposing force comes against those sins. Unless darkness sees the light, how will the darkness be lightened? Repentance breaks the cycle and opens the door for the presence of God. Yes, we apparently can repent for the sins of a land and a people. Ezra did. Daniel did. Jesus did. "Forgive them, Father, for they know not what they do," Jesus said in Luke 23:34.

Jesus also held whole cities responsible for the rejection of the Gospel. He said, "Woe to you, Chorazin! Woe to you, Bethsaida! For if the mighty works which were done in you had been done in Tyre and Sidon, they would have repented long ago, sitting in sackcloth and ashes. But it will be more tolerable for Tyre and Sidon at the judgment than for you" (Luke 10:13-14).

When we understand by research and revelation the sins of our region, it is incumbent upon us to act. If intercession is not made, judgment will be the inevitable result. In Isaiah 21:12, the prophet proclaims, "Someone from among you keeps calling to me: 'Watchman, what of the night? How much time is left?' The watchman replies, 'Your judgment day is dawning now. Turn again to God, so that I can give you better news. Seek for Him, then come and ask again!' We must act and do so with vigor. Earnest intercessory efforts can cause God to avert the judgment He intended. Moses prayed such a prayer and saved a nation because of it.

Scriptural models for spiritual history research are found in both Daniel and Ezra. In modern church terms, they were "spiritual mappers." According to C. Peter Wagner, President of the Global Harvest Ministries and Chancellor of the Wagner Leadership Institute, spiritual mapping is a tool given by God to His people to help break strongholds and reach lost souls for Christ. After much study and research, Daniel "understood by the book of letters" that the Babylonian captivity was nearing its prophesied end. He believed Jeremiah's predictions and began to inform his people. Prayers of repentance and intercessions were made resulting in the overthrow of the captors and the loosing of the captives. Would God have ended the captivity without the prayers and intercession? Probably not. He not only delights in our participation; He often requires it.

Help Break Strongholds

During the years I poured over thousands of pages of documents, books, court records and much more, I was guided by dreams and visions and experienced many divinely appointed meetings and conversations. My work was birthed out of thousands of hours of prayers and tearful pleadings with the Lord for mercy. In June 1998, I was in prayerful intercession when a vision came upon me. I was facing a target from about twenty feet away when suddenly an arrow whisked past my ear and hit the bulls-eye. The Lord spoke, "Time to take down the principality!"

The vision points us to the powerful second purpose for this body of research. According to Victor Lorenzo, a leader in the revival of Resistencia and La Plata, Argentina, "Spiritual mapping combines research, divine revelation and documented evidence in order to provide complete and exact data concerning the identity, strategies and methods employed by spiritual forces of darkness to influence the people and churches of a given region."

We must consider the fact that enemy forces are opposing us. Paul acknowledged this in II Corinthians 4:34, "And even if our gospel is veiled, it is veiled to those who are perishing, in whose case the god of this world has blinded the minds of the unbelieving that they might not see."

The ultimate function of principalities, powers, and spiritual wickedness in high places is to "blind the minds" of the unbelieving to the glorious Gospel of Jesus. Spiritual mapping not only reveals the sins of the people in a certain region, but it reveals the enemies who have been at work in the darkness encouraging the sin and blinding minds from the Gospel.

Why should our region's particular spiritual history be specifically reviewed? We must consider that certain spirits are given power and responsibility over certain geographic regions.

Ministers are well aware that different regions of the United States struggle with differing kinds of sins. Timothy Warner, a former missionary to West Africa and now professor of missions at Trinity Evangelical Divinity School said, "I have come to believe that Satan does indeed assign a demon or corps of demons to every geopolitical unit in the world, and that they are among the principalities and powers against whom we wrestle." Warner adds, "Satan delegates high-ranking members of the hierarchy of evil spirits to control nations, regions, cities, tribes, neighborhoods, and other social networks. Their major assignment is to prevent God from being glorified in their territory which they do by directing the activities of lower-ranking demons."

Much study can be made of the Old Testament evidence that territorial spirits and their dominance of geographical areas are taken for granted as the history of Israel unfolds. "In the New Testament, we must consider the instance of a territorial spirit's power being broken in Paul's encounter with the sorcerer Elymas in eastern Cyprus. Elymas's close association with the proconsul Sergius Paulus, the political authority of the region, suggests a spiritual dominance of the region. When a power encounter breaks the power of Elymas, suddenly Sergius Paulus believes" (Wagner).

Just as each region has territorial spirits assigned to it, each region has prophetic promises given to it by Almighty God. The enemy attempts to prevent the fulfillment of these promises and to rob each region of its God-given destiny. Bethlehem was prophetically designated to bring forth the Messiah. Satanically motivated infanticide attempted to thwart this prophetic destiny. Surely the intercessory prayers of Simeon and Anna and others like them were instrumental in defeating Satan's diabolical plan. What diabolical plans could we thwart?

Preparing For Evangelism

The third and ultimate objective of spiritual mapping is preparing for evangelism—reconciliation of God and man. Averting God's judgment against a given land and people through intercession is essential but not complete. Identifying and employing a strategy for the defeat of enemy forces is also essential. However, the ultimate goal God has in mind for all this activity is saving souls.

A prophet who visited the region in 1998 taught the principle that guides me, "What God reveals He wants to heal." Remember what God promised? "... then will I hear from heaven and will forgive their sin and will heal their land," (II Chronicles 7:14). This is the promise of revival: land healing, people healing, family healing, and government healing.

God promises this in Isaiah 25:7-12:

And He will destroy on this mountain
the surface of the covering cast over all people,
and the veil that is spread over all nations.
He will swallow up death forever,
and the Lord GOD will wipe away tears from all faces;
the rebuke of His people
He will take away from all the earth;
For the LORD has spoken.
And it will be said in that day:
"Behold, this *is* our God;
we have waited for Him, and He will save us.
This *is* the LORD;
we have waited for Him;
we will be glad and rejoice in His salvation."
For on this mountain the hand of the LORD will rest,
And Moab shall be trampled down under Him,
as straw is trampled down for the refuse heap.
And He will spread out His hands in their midst
as a swimmer reaches out to swim,
And He will bring down their pride
Together with the trickery of their hands.
The fortress of the high fort of your walls

He will bring down, lay low,
and bring to the ground, down to the dust.

Aren't multitudes of people coming to the Glorious Christ, the true desire of every Christian? How can it not be? Isn't He lovely? Isn't He altogether beautiful? How can we not be eager to share Him with others?

It is time for the prophetic destiny of our region to be fulfilled. It is time for those who are called to this land and people to ready themselves for a great war and a great victory. We must not be passive and say, "If it is the Lord, He will do it Himself." Paul did not think that way and hazarded his life for the sake of souls. Many of the saints of old understood that God has called us to battle together with Him. That is the whole point of the armor spoken of in Ephesians chapter 6.

However, before we zealously grasp the sword and wade into the battle, we must understand that we cannot do warfare against that which remains inside of us. We have only as much power as we have truth. We cannot repent for regional sins of the past and let those sins remain in us.

Only when we have humbled ourselves so completely, so thoroughly to the cleansing blood of Jesus, only when we have forsaken our own secret sins, only when we have entered into the naked truth of who we really are can we receive the power to destroy the enemy.

Once we are broken, cleansed and made new, we must be wise as serpents. We must be as shrewd as Jesus. We must know our enemy and understand what place we have in the troops as we assemble for war. It is a powerfully deadly work. It is a dangerous and courageous work. It is an eternal work.

CHAPTER THREE

THE LAND OF THE OSAGE

"Every pebble, rock, fish, or floating body either animate or inanimate which occupies the bottom of the stream is seen while passing over it with the most perfect accuracy; and our canoe often seemed as if suspended in air, such is the remarkable transparency of the water."
Henry Rowe Schoolcraft

What a beautiful land we have been given! When I released the first edition of the book, I could not tell for sure what geographic region was part of my assignment. My research seemed to focus on Taney County and the Branson region. However, I am very aware that the heartland region of America, which includes land in Missouri and Arkansas, has many striking similarities: culturally, politically, geographically, and historically. In fact, many of the same stories we have can be found in other communities within our mountains. The names may be different, but the themes are the same.

For that reason, and because of the confirmations I have received since 2004, I believe our region is more than just Branson, Missouri. It is more than just Taney County. It is more than just the White River Valley region. In the last few years I have come to believe that it may be more clearly described as the Land of the Osage.

This magnificent, ancient land is a land of many contrasts. From lush meadows and rich river valleys to rocky high peaks, from trickling brooks to rushing rivers, from the shaggy red cedar to the imposing pine all creation manifests the glory of God and the life of faith it takes to live here. It is a beautiful land, a simple land where commonplace things take on elegance unmatched by the jewels of kings and queens.

Native Ozark poet, Mary Elizabeth Prather Mahnkey, wrote in the 1930s, *Common Things Have Beauty, Charm and Grace:*

I stick smart weed and beggar lice
In with my bouquet
And then I smile
When my friends say,
"How beautiful, how delicate
What can these blossoms be?"
"O yes," I say, "O yes,
But it takes one just like me
To show you all
That common things
Have beauty, charm and grace,
But not until you see them
Stuck in a crystal vase"

Geologists consider our land to be a creation of prehistoric ice age volcanic activity. Shifting plates and churning icebergs are credited with creating the many layers of various rocks so artfully placed and colored that one region of sheer river bluffs cut by the White River was named Calico Rock by early settlers.

In 1818, explorer and adventurer, Henry Rowe Schoolcraft, recorded his encounter with the Ozarks region in a journal that was one of the first glimpses non-Indians had of our land. In his journal, recently republished by Milton Rafferty, Schoolcraft noted many cedar balds and glades and commented on their barren landscape where natural, open areas in the forest reflected a harsh yet fragile environment. Glades are composed of patches of exposed bedrock and shallow, stony soil covered with clumps of tall prairie grasses, wildflowers, desert cacti, and stunted cedar trees. Most hilltop balds and upland glades escaped cultivation due to their poor soils. River valleys supported a dense growth of tall cane (Rafferty).

Our land is a harsh land, an unyielding land, a land that demands diligence and perseverance, but it is also a land of forests and fields, home to a rich variety of trees and vegetation. Valleys and hillsides are thick with cotton-wood, white elm, buckeye, black walnut, white oak, red oak, sugar maple, mulberry, dogwood, sassafras, persimmon, redbud, papaw and wild cherry to name only a few.

The Ozark region is one of America's foremost karst landscapes. Caves are common since these and sinkholes along with bubbling springs form easily in the thick limestone and dolomite formations. The land is rolling and rocky, a patchwork of promise and pain.

In the novel, *The Shepherd of the Hills,* by Harold Bell Wright, Preachin' Bill described his native land:

> When God looked upon th' work of his hand an' called hit good, he war sure a lookin' at this here Ozark country. Rough? Law yes! Hit war made that a way on purpose. Ain't nothin' to a flat country nohow! A man jest naturally wear hisself plumb out a walkin' on the level 'thout ary down hill t' spell him. An' then look how much more there is of hit! Take forty acres o' flat now an' hit's jest a forty, but you take forty acres o' this here Ozark country an' God 'lmighty only

> knows how much ‘twould be if hit war rolled out flat. “Taint no wonder ‘t all, God rested when he made these here hills; he jest naturally had t’ quit, fer he done his beatenest an’ war plumb gin out (Bell Wright).

It is true our land is magnificent in its simplicity, but the real story of the Ozarks is told in its rivers. The Osage Indian tribe dominated the “land between the three rivers: the Missouri to the north, the Mississippi to the east and the Arkansas to the south. The plains of what later became Kansas and Oklahoma served as the western border. Within these boundaries are several beautiful threads of God’s glory: the Pomme De Terre and the Merrimac to the northeast, the Osage to the northwest, the Eleven Point to Missouri’s southeast, and the Buffalo to the south.

However, it is the White River which sews Missouri and Arkansas together in a meandering thread of gleaming crystal. Of the White River, Schoolcraft wrote:

> It is so clear, white, and transparent, that the stones and pebbles in its bottom, at the depth of eight or ten feet are reflected through it with the most perfect accuracy as to color, size, and position, and at the same time appear as if within two or three feet of the surface. Its depth cannot therefore be judged by the eye with any probability of that degree of exactness which can be had by looking into common clear streams. The explanation of this phenomenon is referable to the extreme degree of the purity of the water, which holds no fine particles of earth in suspension, and admits the rays of light to pass

through it without being intercepted or refracted by those particles (Rafferty).

From its waters, Schoolcraft enjoyed an optical feast. He called it an enchanting river:

> ...with a smooth and gentle flow, and the most imposing, diversified, and delightful scenery. Its shores are composed of smooth, spherical, and angular pieces of opaque, red, and white gravel, consisting of water-worn fragments of carbonate of lime, hornstone, quartz, and jasper. Every pebble, rock, fish, or floating body either animate or inanimate which occupies the bottom of the stream is seen while passing over it with the most perfect accuracy; and our canoe often seemed as if suspended in air, such is the remarkable transparency of the water. Sometimes the river for many miles washed the base of a wall of calcareous rock, rising to an enormous height, and terminating in spiral, broken, and miniform masses, in the fissures of which the oak and cedar had forced their crooked roots, and hung in a threatening posture above us. Perched upon these the eagle, hawk, turkey, and heron surveyed our approach without alarm. Facing such rocks, the corresponding curve of the river, invariably presented a level plain of rich alluvial soil covered with a vigorous growth of forest-trees along with shrubs and vines, and affording a most striking contrast to the sterile grandeur of the opposite shore (Rafferty).

Through the Ozarks, beautiful White River has been dammed three times. In 1913 Powersite Dam was built to produce hydroelectric power for the region. This provided for the creation of what is now known as Taneycomo Lake, a premier trout fishing lake. The name is derived from combining the syllables in Taney County, Missouri. In 1958 Table Rock Dam was completed producing Table Rock Lake which extends 79 miles upstream and created 800 miles of shoreline. Bull Shoals Dam impounds the White River one last time before water travels to the mouth of the Mississippi River. It was completed in 1951 and dedicated by President Harry Truman in 1952.

In 1994, I wrote a piece for the *Branson Living Magazine*. As things turned out, I began to understand it may have been prophetic prose from the Holy Spirit.

> I'm perching on the shoreline of the White listening to the voices of time flowing from the belly of the river. Fall has kissed the Ozarks and although it's much too chilly, I dangle my bare feet in the rippling water, listening. I can barely hear the story, the old, old, story which sounds faintly like a song. It fades in and out like sounds from the aged transistor radio I used to hide under my pillow at night as a child.
>
> The story of the Branson region begins. It is whispered, sometimes shouted, often sung and I'm listening to the river tell it to me now.
>
> The White River flowed unimpeded for centuries, carving out its relentless passageway through the mountains. Heralding from Arkansas, it visits Missouri only briefly, then returns to its native land. The Osage borrowed from the White

only what they needed and remained proud caretakers of the land until they relinquished their rights in the Osage Treaty of 1808. Ten years later Schoolcraft and his companions explored the tangled shorelines of the unruly water and wrote of its crystalline beauty.

Emigration occurred shortly after and by 1840, Jesse Jennings' census revealed just over 3,000 residents of this harshly magnificent one thousand square miles. Homesteads were hacked from rock and cedar and the river ran through it all. Listen.

Settlers settled and neighbors were neighborly, sometimes more for the necessity of it all rather than in response to Christian commands. Then the war came in 1861.

The river wanted nothing to do with it and told her people who agreed for there wasn't anything to be won or lost by it all here along the shores of the White. But the armies came anyway and took the guileless and ruthless side by side, men and boys, and the river cried in agony with the women and children. Nothing could be done, however, so the river ran through it all.

Time marched on and so did some of the Stone and Taney County men and not-so-boys back to their devastated land. They touched base at the shore of the rippling waterway, shuddering at the distant sounds of change. Others were leaving their city-shattered lives looking for Utopia and yearning for the sounds of the river. Listen.

Autumn's chill is too much. I pull my now blue feet from the water and tuck them underneath me shivering, still listening.

Land heretofore unattended, seeming to belong to no one and everyone suddenly sprouted a homestead and a stranger. The magnificent tanglewood seemed much too revealing, and those who were born naked and helpless in this wild land felt uncomfortably uncovered. The river clashed with the stubborn rocks in narrow passageways as natives and strangers eyed each other warily. But the river ran through it all.

Then in 1884 the Baldknobbers came. Might and right both took a poke in the nose and neither liked it one bit. Some strangers left and some natives did too while the sounds of the river echoed plaintively in their ears.

Big Nat Kinney was a mighty man, about as right as might could be. But he fell and the earth shook and the people were astonished when they saw their reflections in the White for they didn't like what they could see. Listen.

A sound came through the mountains, more like a thunder, a rumble and roar and smoke belched from her smokestack and Progress was here.

She wore fine, fine clothes and had a lovely parasol and a purse which the natives admired and so bit by bit she traded them for their land. Towns were born where they never were meant to be. The river was laid bare and anxiously fretting her future kept climbing out of her banks making a nuisance of herself to the people.

Someone needed a light. The sun and the moon were not enough so the river was powerfully dammed. Part of her became a lake. Commerce shot the rapids and landed in the middle of the lake while the river ran through it all. Listen.

Bell Wright had come and gone and shuddered for what he had done but the floodgates were opened and villages became towns yearning to become cities.

The people loved their river and loved her lake and proudly showed her off like a shiny penny won after a game of marbles in the hot summer sun. Still the river was growing old and cranky. She sometimes slapped at those she loved. She was dammed again. Listen.

Like a dying woman after a blood transfusion she was energized and became deep and wide and beautiful in her old age. The people hated her and loved her marveling at the great white bandage upon her belly. When she felt better, she sat up to eat at Table Rock.

So did the people. A man came and another city-town was born on the quiet side of the lake. To the east, trout played where catfish once wallowed, but the bass were good no matter how or where you sliced them. And the river ran through it all.

The cave that was once a secret garden was no longer a secret anymore and we were proud of that. Progress was still living in town and had long since put up her parasol and purse for she wanted instead things that looked simply lovely.

The river was much different now because she was twice a lake, then thrice a lake and it was too confusing to all the busy people. And anyway strangers had come again. The natives wagged their hoary heads and wished they'd just leave money instead. But cities had shattered the strangers' lives and their ears, full of din, yearned for the sounds of the river. Listen.

It was possible now, even probable that the towns would become cities. Then wafting over the leafy hillsides a new sound was heard. This was music like no front porch on a Saturday night. The people loved the new music and the new musicians who were so much like themselves. And the musical strangers touched the blue water of the river-lake and loved her too. More musical strangers came and touched too and the river ran through it all. Listen.

Over the hill then came a new sound, music-like but with a bit too much clinking. The strangers and the natives shook their heads wondering. But the sound faded in and out and was too hard to interpret. Listen.

The strangers and the natives often couldn't tell each other apart clapping each other upon the shoulders and laughing at their children growing. Listen.

A sound nagged at the back of their minds but they were full of life and the living of it while the river ran through it all. Listen.

The sound became a noise. The noise clanked loudly like heavy coins in a noisy bar. The strangers and the natives are alarmed when suddenly a deluge of new strangers strode along the river-lake in Italian shoes and silk suits with chirping phones. Listen.

The game of marbles was suddenly over. Innocence was gone and speculative strangers sucked up the land like ice cream through a straw. A chill shadow fell over the hillsides. Foreheads became wrinkled overnight as natives and strangers alike tried to figure out the rules to this new game they didn't want to learn how to play. Listen.

But Progress plugged in her radio and television and flopped down a newspaper in front of the people. They must play or be played upon. The river wondered that no one touched her waters much anymore. Listen.

Projects popped like popcorn in a microwave instead of like shoots of tender grasses in the warm summer sun. The river-lake hunched her shoulders still not ready for the blow. And boy did she blow! Blow by blow by blow by blow. Then the storm quieted and the strangers, natives, and new strangers stood looking at one another warily. Listen.

The river-lake weathered the storm like she does so well. The sun hesitantly peeped over the mountains. The people looked anew at the water and drawn to her sparkling shores, they reached down and touched it. And the river runs through us all.

CHAPTER FOUR

THE FIRST PEOPLE-THE OSAGE

"...the most religious tribe of all North American tribes..." Garrick Bailey

As I was researching, looking for clues that would help me uncover the principality that ruled over our region, I decided to begin with a look at the first people. After all, they were the ones through whom territorial spirits could and did govern. The Osage Indians ruled supreme in the land between the three rivers. However, just four years after the 1804 purchase of the Louisiana Territory, the tribe reluctantly treatied their land to the United States government. European immigrants were pushing for new lands to settle in Kentucky and Tennessee. The government looked at the obvious choice, the wild lands west of the Mississippi, into which they could relocate the displaced woodland tribes such as Kickapoo, Shawnee, Delaware, and most especially, the Cherokee. The displaced Osage would be replaced by the displaced woodland tribes.

The Osage territory was described in the Treaty of Fort Clark:

"Beginning at Fort Clark (Fort Osage, now Sibly, Missouri) on the Missouri (river), five miles above Fire Prairie, and running thence a due south course to the river Arkansaw (sic) and down the same to the Mississippi."

On the surface the treaty of 1808 seemed to be a properly executed agreement, however, the Osage maintained for several decades that they had not given up hunting rights. This caused several serious conflicts with the immigrant tribes as well as white settlers and the squatters who invaded Cherokee treaty land. On December 9, 1824, the Missouri Legislature passed a law "to restrain intercourse (trade) with Indians within the State of Missouri." This was one of the efforts to force the tribes to stay out of Missouri. By the late 1830s most of Missouri was void of Osage.

There were several recorded Osage villages in the land that later became Taney County. Earliest fur traders noted significant villages at the mouth of Swan Creek near what is now Forsyth, Missouri (Shadow Rock Park). Another Osage village was at the mouth of the James River, near Galena, Missouri in what is now Stone County. Villages were often scattered along the White River. Rockaway Beach and Branson are also locations where villages were located.

According to Elmo Ingenthron's *Indians of the Ozarks Plateau:*

> The Osage warriors were of remarkable height, not many being less than six feet high and many much taller. They were well-formed, athletic, agile and robust. Instances of deformity and insanity were rare among them. They bore sickness and pain with great fortitude, seldom uttering a complaint. The Osages of both sexes often tattooed different parts of their bodies and wore different facial paints associated with war, death, religion and hunting.

Ingenthron recorded that the Osages had "long been imbued with a burning ambition to be the super-race men preeminent who walked on mother earth. They were more successful than other tribes at avoiding the destruction caused by whiskey sellers. In their long struggle for greatness their progress had seldom been thwarted by deformity, insanity, or suicide which was more characteristic of a weaker race."

Pride was an important characteristic of the Osage. Why not? They were the tallest, strongest, and fiercest of any tribe. The primary objective of marriage among the Osage was warrior perfection and long life for individuals in the tribe. For that reason, the strongest, most beautiful brides were married to young warriors of proven and unquestionable bravery and physical fitness. The strongest bred with the strongest. Weakness was despised and rejected. In fact, Osage men who proved to have no stomach for the butchery of war were forced to wear women's clothing and refused the right to marry. They lived out their life in shame and humiliation (Ingenthron).

Once the magnificent warrior was married to his wife, he became heir to all his wife's sisters whom he could espouse as additional wives to bear his children or he could choose to give them as gifts to others. By this act, the Osage reasoned they could maintain the strength of their tribe. Marriage outside the tribe was largely shunned and those who chose to do so faced serious consequences. Pure blood and pure breeding were the consummate goals of matrimony.

This practice was instrumental in the fall of the Osage's power in the early 1800s. Woodland tribes who had been pushed out of their native homelands east of the Mississippi made their way into Osage territory and faced the fierce wrath of their warriors. However, there were casualties on both sides and the Osage began to dwindle in number.

The religious beliefs of the Osage included reverence for Wakanda, or Wah-Kon-Tah, which was the term used for deity. There were seven great Wakandas—Darkness, the Upper World, the Ground, the Thunder-being, the Sun, the Moon and the Morning Star. The Upper World was perhaps the greatest of the Wakandas, and in some of the tribes it was the supreme Wakanda. There was no set form of worship of Wakanda. Every one thought Wakanda dwelt in some secret place. It was believed that THE Wakanda or some Wakanda was ever present to hear any petition or prayer for help. Wakandas may be more clearly understood by the Caucasian to mean, "forces." There were many forms of propitiation, or these may have been sometimes in the nature of invocations, such as the elevation and the lowering of the arms, the presentation of the mouth-piece of the pipe, the emission of the smoke, the burning of cedar needles in the sweat house, the application of the major terms of kinship, ceremonial waiting, sacrifice and offerings, and the cutting of the body with knives.

The Osage called the sun the "mysterious one of the day," and prayed to Wakanda as Grandfather. Prayer was always made toward the sun without regard to its position in the heavens. Here is an Osage prayer:

> Ho, Mysterious Power, you who are the Sun! Here is tobacco! I wish to follow your course. Grant that it may be so! Cause me to meet whatever is good (for my advantage) and to give a wide berth to anything that may be to my injury or disadvantage. Throughout this island (world) you regulate everything that moves, including human beings. When you decide for

> one that his last day on earth has come, it is so. It can not be delayed. Therefore, O Mysterious Power, I ask a favor of you (Ingenthron).

The Pleiades, the Belt of Orion, the Morning Star, the Small Star, the Bowl of the Dipper, are all Wakandas, and they are addressed as "Grandfather." While the Wakandas are considered forces helpful to the native people, the Osage believed there were beings that are considered hostile and were greatly feared. In the Siouan and Osage tongue, Wakandagi, as a noun, means a subterranean or water monster, a large horned reptile mentioned in the myths, and still supposed to dwell beneath the bluffs along the Missouri river (Dorsey). Just the thought of this water monster was enough to send icy chills into the veins of even the bravest warrior. This grave fear inspired numerous ritual supplications to Wakandas for protection from the terrors of this being. River travel sparked trepidation so the Osage chose to remain within the boundaries of the great rivers of the Missouri, Mississippi and Arkansas.

The Osage carefully observed their religious traditions and permitted few things to interrupt their devotion. The "dawn chant" practiced by the Osage, was probably handed down to them from their Siouan ancestors. This manifestation of religious worship drew the interest and attention of all the early explorers and fur traders who encountered it. Ingenthron wrote:

> Where ever the Osages pitched their camps the coming dawn brought this strange, emotion packed, religious phenomenon. In preparation for the ritual, they sometimes anointed their faces with mud from the bosom of mother earth. Their prayers began in the highest singsong note

> obtainable and continued for as long as there was breath, in a progressively lower tone to the lowest key. This was repeated over and over again until they were wrought into a pitch. Some perhaps chanted the death song for some deceased love one. Others may have chanted the hunter's song or sought Wah-Kon-Tah's favors for some upcoming slave or horse stealing expedition. Some lay prostrate upon the ground, exhausted, crying and sobbing as if their hearts were broken.

Perhaps no one but the Osage could describe their morning chant, and they even had trouble doing so. Osage John Joseph Mathews in an excerpt from his book, *The Osages*, expressed it this way:

> I heard it many times later as I grew up until the time I entered high school, and I have never been able to describe it to myself. It was indescribable and there is nothing with which to compare it. It filled my little boy's soul with fear and bitter-sweetness, an exotic yearning, and when it had ended and I lay there in my exultant fear-trance, I hoped there would be more of it and yet was afraid there might be. It seemed to me later, after I had begun to reason, that this prayer, this change, this soul-stirring petition, always ended before it was finished, in a sob of frustration.

Another religious practice often dealt with the tattooing of the spider on the backside of a young woman's hand on her wedding day. This was a prominent mark of distinction among first class families for it took many horses, robes and blankets to afford an artist for the job. To perform the ceremony of the spider tattoo, the artist placed charcoal from the sacred redbud on the back of the maiden's hand, pricked out the geometrical figure of the spider with a wing-bone tattoo needle and rubbed the charcoal into the opening of the skin. The intricate design would last a lifetime. It was the symbol of the Grand Hankah and all the mysterious powers related to it. The Grand Hankah was the mystery lodge which held all the power of the tribe and admittance to it was a serious and secret affair.

Each Osage wedding ceremony was a grand manifestation of symbolism and religious mystery. Burial ceremonies were equally ritualistic. Osage had a particular way of preparing their dead warriors for the resurrection of the spirit. According to Ingenthron:

> To assure a proper ascent of the spirit, the dead warrior was dressed in full battle array with all his war paints brightly shining and all honorary symbols properly displayed. He was then taken to some place of higher elevation and propped upright in a sitting position where he was exposed to the views of Grandfather Sun as he rose in the eastern sky. If Grandfather Sun recognized the warrior and approved of his spirit's ascent, the spirit left the body at exactly noon, or when the sun was directly overhead. If Grandfather Sun failed to recognize the warrior or disapproved of him, his spirit was condemned to earth where it usually took up its abode in the body of a screech owl. As the condemned spirit suffered, its weeping and wailing could be heard at night when its host flitted about the woodlands.

This religious belief, as could be expected, produced great fear in the tribe during the night when it was thought disturbed spirits through woodland owls would wreck havoc on the lives of the living.

Once the Osage was properly buried, the ceremony of mourning did not end. One significant element of mourning was the preparation for revenge. Osage believed the only way to assure their loved one acceptance by Grandfather Sun was to exact revenge as quickly as possible. When an Osage died, someone else had to die as well. Revenge could as easily be paid by the death of a tribal enemy or if the enemy did not fall into their hands, a slave or inferior Osage would do. Many early trappers and settlers unwittingly paid the price of revenge for an Osage warrior killed in battle.

Osage were led by two chiefs, each representing a grand division in the tribe. The Tzi Sho represented peace. The Hunkah represented war. Perhaps one of the most unique aspects of Osage tribal religion was the assembly of "Little Old Men." Carl Chapman discussed this unusual distinction in his book, *Indians and Archaeology of Missouri*. "The powers of the chiefs were limited. They were the leaders of the council rather than the rulers, in regard to decisions concerning civil functions. The true governing body seems to have been the assembly of "Little Old Men," a council of men who had taken the seven degrees in the secret or religious society of the tribe." Ritual knowledge and authority were divided among 24 clan priesthoods. Each clan's priesthood was in turn divided into 7 degrees, each degree associated with a specific segment of the clan's ritual knowledge and authority.

Women were also initiated into the secret society of the Osages. The officiating man of the council gave her four sips of water, symbolizing the river flowing by the tree of life, and then he rubbed her from head to foot with cedar needles, three times in front, three times on her back, and three times on each side, twelve times in all, pronouncing the sacred name of Wakanda as he made each pass. In the Osage tradition, cedar symbolized the tree of life.

Ingenthron remarked on the dominance of the secret society revealed by the way a typical permanent Osage village was created:

> At the height of Osage village planning there were provisions made for each of the two grand divisions, with the Tzi-Sho on the north and the Hunkah on the south of a clear avenue or thoroughfare running east and west between them. The lodges of the two division chiefs were in the center of the village opposite each other with the main avenue between them. All the dwellings of each division were built on their appropriate side of the main avenue arranged in rows, usually of seven lodges to the row with their doors all facing the east.

"The Mystery Lodge of the Osages," was usually built a short distance from the main dwellings of the tribe and frequently was covered with the most beautiful skins available. In the center of the enclosure were a fireplace and a line running east and west representing the path of Grandfather Sun. The mystery lodge housed the governing body of the tribe that included the "Little Old Men" and the two division chiefs. The Tzi-Sho, representing peace, was seated near the center on the north side of the path of Grandfather Sun.

Chapman acknowledges other important officials were the Marmatons—town criers, grand chamberlains, and principal cooks for the chiefs. They were highly respected personages and often were warriors who had lost their families, had been injured or were too old to carry arms.

In a book entitled, *The Osage and the Invisible World*, author Garrick Bailey wrote extensively of Osage religion and ritual. The Osage were known as the most religious tribe of all North American tribes. Rituals ruled their lives.

The Osage religion was not concerned with death and the afterlife. They had only vague concepts of what happened to a person's spirit after death although they believed in a spirit's existence after death. The purpose and focus of their religious was the survival and perpetuity of the Osage people. Of primary concern was the maintenance of their population. Longevity and children were the blessings of Wakanda, and Osage daily life was structured as a ritual to present a never-ending appeal for Wakanda's blessing.

The most direct and immediate physical threat to the Osage's well-being and survival came from other peoples. The Osages saw the world as filled with enemy peoples who could at any time strike and destroy them without warning. As a result, warfare and unity of action were recurrent themes in their religious life.

Although the Osages had rituals that would be classified as fertility rituals, these ceremonies were concerned with children and descendents and were parts of the generalized appeals for Wa-Kon-da's blessings.

Osage religious practices did not emphasize personal supernatural contact. They did not have named gods or goddesses with physical forms. As a result, their rituals did not include masked dancers representing supernatural beings. In the "living world" the realm for which humans bore primary responsibility, unity, war, and peace were of the highest concern.

The Osage priests deliberately restricted knowledge. True knowledge of the meaning of a particular song group was limited only to the priests of the clan who owned it. To protect their knowledge, the priests made extensive use of metaphors in their songs and wi'-gi-e to hide their true meanings. In other cases they deliberately corrupted the words to make them unintelligible (Bailey).

Osage religious beliefs were not based on divine revelation. Most religious beliefs were derived from empirical observations of natural phenomena and from reasoning. Because they were consciously created by humans, religious beliefs, institutions, and rituals were subject to periodic revision by humans in response to changes they perceived in the world of the living. The Osages were not unanimous in their interpretations of religious rituals, and not all supernatural phenomena were integrated into their formal religion (Bailey).

Like all native peoples the Osage were afraid of evil spirits. The women and girls bathed in the streams and anointed themselves with perfume made from horse mint, calamus or columbine seed; all of which were believed to aid them in doing away with evil. The Osage were both superstitious and curious. Any new or strange whistling sounds were attributed to spirits or ghosts and created great fear in the people. French fur traders often sang songs and laughed or whistled. This caused great concern in the natives for they could never be sure when the traders might start whistling or what the outcome might be.

They were afraid of lightning and considered it the act of a grcat and powerful spirit who occasionally struck at the earth in anger splintering or splitting trees. They would never use the wood from trees that had been struck by lightning lest it bring them evil or bad luck. To this day, native Ozarkers practice this same sort of superstition.

Not all supernatural phenomena recognized by the Osages were integrated into their formal religion They held other beliefs that might best be called "folk beliefs"—including belief in prophets, were-animals, witchcraft, "little people," and ghosts. The vast majority of Osages, including the priests, truly believed in the existence of these supernatural phenomena.

There were among the Osages women and men who had the ability to foretell the future. In dreams or visions—the distinction is not always clear—these prophets would see or sense something that was going to occur. Most commonly they warned of impending enemy attacks. Such prophecies were readily validated when a hidden enemy raiding party was discovered. The last and most famous of these prophets was Wa-tian-kah, whose Delphic-like predictions were interpreted as having foretold the Osage's eventual wealth because of oil, the coming of peyote, and even the automobile and airplane.

Some people were thought to have the power to change themselves into animals. One man reportedly was able to transform himself into a snake; in other cases, men could change into deer. Although no known cases were recorded in which people could change themselves into wolves or birds or other life forms, the potential for doing so existed. No explanation is recorded as to why some people had this ability.

There were Osage witches, however, individuals who used supernatural powers to harm others. It is not known whether the Osages recognized one or several categories of witches. There were individuals who prepared various love medicines. There were some malevolent people who could and did harm or even kill others. At least some witches were call “snakes” or “bean shooters,” the latter because they killed others by magically shooting them with mescal beans (Bailey).

The Osages also believed in little people, or mi’-a-gthu-shka. Little people were said to look just like other humans but to be only the size of children. They had their own villages, trails, and other places they frequented. There was a supernatural quality about the little people. Some Osages thought that they could be seen only when they wanted to be seen or were taken unawares. Because the little people were considered potentially dangerous, most Osages avoided contact with them.

The Osages also believed in ghosts. They distinguished fictional tales from stories based on fact, and La Flesche (the early researcher Bailey quotes) recorded a number of Osage ghost stories that were told as true. In them, ghosts did not return from the dead; rather, ghosts of individuals remained among the living for a time after death.

According to Bailey, the Osage were well known among the prairie tribes for cutting off the heads of their enemies. It may well be if the demonic principality that darkened the minds of our first people is not destroyed in this region, it will attract the attention of the anti-Christ spirit that works in the deceived Muslims. The anti-Christ spirit seems to have a penchant for cutting off heads.

Osage beliefs and customs give us a unique look into mindsets that have formed our region’s history. Watch these themes develop; religious rituals/superstitions, the pride of secret societies and racial supremacy, and the bondage of religion and revenge. As you read, you may be prompted to examine your own hcart and mind and see if any of these themes are working in your life.

CHAPTER FIVE

THE CHEROKEE CALLED IT.....Nunna dual Tsuny

(Trail Where They Cried)

VISION OF CHEROKEE SPIRIT OF MURDER

Notes from my personal journal
Sunday Evening, July 12, 1998
Oak Ridge Full Gospel Church, Taney County, Missouri

Sunday Evening, July 12, at the end of the service, Pastor asked us to all go to the walls of the sanctuary the direction in which we lived and pray over our area. Steve (my husband) and I went to the southeast corner pointing toward Kirbyville. I began to pray for Kirbyville. Almost immediately, I was released from that prayer by the Holy Spirit and began instead to pray for Merriam Woods, Rockaway Beach and Forsyth. After a time of intercession, I saw a vivid vision of a group of Native Americans dancing around a fire. In my heart I felt it was a war dance. Suddenly, I saw a gray misty looking figure waft from the fire. In my spirit I knew it was the spirit of murder being sent out from the ritual dance.

I saw the dancers vividly. They had painted circles of red around one eye and black around the other eye. They each gripped a red club in one hand and a black club in the other. I saw a group of Shamans in full headgear in a group to one side. I knew they were praying curses onto the land and whoever lived there. I felt in my spirit that this land was Merriam Woods because that's what I was praying over when the vision began. Suddenly in my mind came "burial grounds." I wondered if this had to do with the Trail of Tears.

Later, I became aware that another lady was knelt before the same wall in deep intercession. It came into my mind that perhaps she was also of Cherokee descent. After the service, I asked to speak with her. I began to tell her what had happened. Her husband came over and sat with us. As I talked, I was overcome with weeping again and saw the whole vision over again. I finished telling her and her husband what I had seen, then suddenly I blurted out, "The spirit of murder will manifest this week in Merriam Woods, Rockaway Beach or Forsyth. I don't know exactly when or exactly where, but this week someone is going to die."

Late that night, Justin Michael Wyman, 20, Forsyth, shot himself to death east of Forsyth. Justin's parents live and own a business across the street from the business owned by the couple to whom I had prophesied those words.

Years later, I read in John Ehle's book, *Trail of Tears,* "He (John Ridge) and his father visited the war dancers who had painted vermilion on their faces, a red circle around one eye, a black circle around the other. Their dance was slow, insistent. Most of the warriors who danced wielded black and red clubs-the colors of fearlessness and blood."

We call it...
TRAIL OF TEARS

From John Ehle's, *Trail of Tears:*

> O.I.C. (Officer in Charge) Fort Hetzel, GA: To H.Q. (Headquarters) "commenced on May 26, 1838 in securing the Indians, 425 or perhaps 450."
>
> June 3, 1838. Col. Bynum, HQ Cheowa Valley, "the collection of Cherokee Indians preparatory to the emigration will commence in Cheowa Valley on tomorrow morning...."
>
> June 4, 1838. Col. Bynum, HQ Fort Montgomery to Gen. Scott, "....I am desirous of knowing whether there are particular instructions to be given as to the manner of disposing of the property of the Indians, whether they are to be marched off.....and their property taken care of afterwards?" (Ehle)

Much has been written of this terrible chapter in America's history. Little has been written of Taney County's part. Even before President Andrew Jackson betrayed his word to the Cherokee people that "you shall remain in your ancient land as long as grass grows and water runs," tribal members had begun removal west of the Mississippi.

The Keetoowah (Western Cherokee or Old Settlers) had their origin with a small group of pro-French Cherokee which relocated to northern Arkansas, southern and southeastern Missouri after the French defeat by the British in 1763. The Spanish welcomed them and granted land. Towards the end of the American Revolution in 1782, they were joined by a group of pro-British Cherokee. With the migration of the Chickamauga (1794-

99), the Keetoowah became formidable and a threat to the Osage who originally claimed the territory. Cherokee and Osage warfare was fairly common in 1803 when the United States gained control of the area through the Louisiana Purchase. With continued migration, the Western Cherokee steadily gained at the expense of the Osage, and by 1808 over 2,000 Cherokee were established in northern Arkansas.

The Turkey Town treaty (1817) was the first formal recognition of the Western Cherokee by the United States. Under its terms, 4,000 Cherokee ceded their lands in Tennessee in exchange for a reservation with the Western Cherokee in northwest Arkansas and Southwest Missouri. Several bands had settlements on Bear Creek near Harrison, Arkansas just south of Branson in the 1820s.

During Schoolcraft's 1818 exploration of the Ozarks, he wrote, "Some excitement prevails among the people occupying the right bank of the White River on account of the recent treaty concluded with the Cherokee Indians. By it those Indians relinquish certain tracts of land in the state of Tennessee, but are to receive in exchange the lands lying between the north bank of the Arkansaw (sic), and the south bank of the White River. Those people therefore who have located themselves upon the right bank of the river and improved farms are now necessitated to relinquish them which is considered a piece of injustice" (Rafferty).

With this new immigration during 1818-19, the number of Western Cherokee swelled to over 6,000. However, the Osage continued to object to the Cherokee presence, and the Americans were forced to build Fort Smith (1817) and Fort Gibson (1824) to maintain peace. White settlers who refused to move and those encroaching on the treatied land were soon demanding the removal of both the Cherokee and Osage. In 1824, the Missouri Legislature passed a law making it illegal for Indians to remain in the state. Confusion existed on whether this pertained to mixed bloods as well. Under intense political pressure, in 1828 the Western Cherokee finally agreed to exchange their Arkansas lands for a new location in Oklahoma. The boundaries were finally determined in 1833, although it took until 1835 to get Osage agreement.

Those Cherokee east of the Mississippi, many who were men of letters and learning, and who did not believe their native lands would ever be stripped from them awoke to a harsh reality in May of 1838. The Georgia Guard, which consisted of mostly white European settlers, greedy with the lust of the Georgia Gold Rush, gave their hands heartily to the forced removal of Cherokee from their state. They were aided by troops from Alabama, Florida, North and South Carolina, and Tennessee. Tribal members were force marched to forts and holding pens throughout these regions and held for months in the most base and miserable conditions.

Although no measurable amount of gold was ever found on native lands, the immigrant settlers profited nicely from the large, beautiful plantations, and cleared and developed lands the Cherokee had once owned. Fourteen "detachments" of Cherokee were officially removed by troops and private contractors and marched to Oklahoma. I believe three of the later detachments traveled through Taney County in the Missouri Ozarks.

June 6, 1838. Nathaniel Smith, Ross' Landing to Gen. Scott, "This morning I started a party of near 1,000...Lt. Deas was to take 1,000 or so on flatboats going as far as he could by water" (Ehle). On the 9th, the group reached Decatur and Deas hired passage on a railroad to

Tuscumbia where the water would be deeper. The train could carry half the group at a time. 100 escaped to return home. At Tuscumbia many of the male Indians were gone. Deas believed a total of 311 had escaped. No one died in this first detachment that included Principal Chief John Ross. Immediately upon his arrival in Indian Territory, he petitioned to contract with the government to administrate the removal using his brother Lewis as the actual contractor. His petition was granted. The following 13 detachments were "Cherokee administered" under the watchful eye of the Army.

The second detachment headed out in June. 875 were under the watch of Lt. R.H.K. Whitely. Of the 875 who left Tennessee, only 602 arrived, the others were dead or had escaped fleeing into caves and mountains. The detachment arrived August 1, at Lee's Creek near Indian Territory (now Oklahoma).

The third band started June 17, 1838. There were an estimated 1,070. Men, women and children traveled by foot and wagon 160 miles to Waterloo, AL. There they were boarded on flatboats. Before boarding, the Cherokee had petitioned, "to wait for cooler weather." Superintendent Smith determined they should go on. "Shortly after which about 300 of them, threw a part of their baggage out of the wagons, took it and broke for the woods...." At Little Rock, only 722 of the original 1,070 remained.

June 18, 1838. Nathaniel Smith, Superintendent of Cherokee Emigration received from Gen. Scott upon petition by 100 prominent Cherokee, permission to suspend removal until September 1 (Ehle).

The journey was tortuous in many ways. "Most of the Cherokee were superstitious. They considered rivers, even small creeks to be ways to the underworld; pools were basins of UKTENA, a serpent with supernatural powers. To take a river trip was every hour threatening, to undertake any journey might annoy the spirits left here at home and would certainly alert new ones, with prospects of torture and terror. Also, west was the direction taken by the spirits of the dead" (Ehle).

August 28, 1838. William Shorey Coodey, a nephew to John Ross (Principal Chief of the Cherokee) witnessed:

> The line of wagons was ready. It was noon. At this very moment a low sound of distant thunder fell on my ear. In almost an exact western direction a dark spiral cloud was rising above the horizon and sent forth a murmur. I almost fancied a voice of divine indignation, for the wrong of my poor and unhappy countrymen, driven by brutal power from all they loved and cherished in the land of their fathers, to gratify the cravings of avarice. The sun was unclouded—no rain fell—the thunder rolled away and sounds hushed in the distance. The scene around and before me and in the elements above was peculiarly impressive and singular. It was at once spoken of by several persons near me, and looked upon as omens of some future event in the west (Ehle).

On the first day of September another detachment was forced out consisting of 859 persons. Two days later, a detachment of 846 natives moved westward. The drought and brutal heat continued. No rain fell until September 23 when a light-refreshing shower occurred. Suddenly, on September 28, it rained. The drought was finally broken.

Although Lewis Ross, brother of Principal Chief John Ross, had contracted with the government to oversee the removal, he was busy attending to his own fortunes. He chartered a boat in 1838 and transported his slaves from Georgia to the Cherokee Nation. An armed guard met the boat and escorted his property to his plantation for sale to other Cherokee who had no compunctions about slavery.

Back on the trail, Cherokee were enduring incredible hardships. Troops and Lewis Ross's own "contractors" had stolen much of the government issued provisions including food and blankets. Wagons that the government had commissioned to carry the natives never arrived. There was one white doctor for every 1,000 Cherokee. Dr. Elizur Butler, an American Board Medical Missionary served on the Trail. "From the first of June I have felt I have been in the midst of death," he wrote. He estimated that 1/5 had died. "And of the blacks? How many of the dead were black (slaves)? Nobody troubled to guess."

Cherokee religious rituals were in shambles during the brutal marches. Shamans believed they must stay with a corpse three days and three nights to ward off witches with their own voices, their chants, until the soul, after the three days and nights could make his escape to the next world. "But the march must continue; there are no days to attend the graves. Think of that, all these corpses with their souls still inside, are being left for the robbery of the witches" (Cherokee Shaman).

Cape Girardeau, Missouri, was the staging ground for the journey west of the Mississippi. The route followed what was known as The Virginia Warriors Path which led across the Cumberland Mountains, to the falls of the Ohio and across what is now southern Indiana and Illinois, to the Mississippi, and west through southern

Missouri to the Rocky Mountains. It probably crossed the Mississippi near what is now Gray's Point and also at Grand Tower, then followed Apple Creek, or the dividing ridge between the waters of the St. Francis and Meramec rivers. The lower trail would hug the edge of the great alluvial St. Francis Basin, gradually ascending by way of Otter, Big Barren and Pike creeks to the plateau of the Ozarks.

Substantially on this route, a railroad is now in operation. This trail extends through the counties of Carter, Shannon, Howell, the southwest corner of Texas, and southern Webster, to what is now Springfield near the center of Greene County, then traveling southwest through McDonald county into Oklahoma.

The "Wire," or Fayetteville Road, follows, in the main, one of the Indian trails to the southwest down Wilson's Creek and the James River to one of the White River hunting grounds. It is probable that the Delaware and Kickapoo followed a trail that passed due south of Springfield about a mile west of the "Wilderness" road. The Osages, it is certain, followed another trail to their hunting ground on the White river, a road now partially outlined by the Chadwick branch of the 'Frisco railroad. The trail journeyed past Sequiota Park (Fisher's Cave), through Galloway along the road to the ford below the bridge which crosses the James. From there it continued on to about a mile south of the bridge, where the old Linden Road begins, following the latter in a general course southeast toward Chadwick, then down Swan Creek to Forsyth, or the mouth of Big Beaver Creek. Following the Wire Road, another Osage trail branched, from the beginning of the Linden Road southward down to Bull Creek and on to the White River.

By the time the last groups of Cherokee, many consisting of mixed-bloods traveled through the Kickapoo plains (where Springfield is now) it was void of food supplies. Precious deer, turkey, nuts and berries and anything else the natives could forage for their survival had to be gathered to sustain life. Latter removal groups had secured permission to be removed by contract workers. Weary, cold and hungry themselves, they permitted a detour through Christian County near Finley Creek, south to Bull Creek near Rockaway Beach and westward along the White River through Taney County. Here the tanglewood offered ample hiding places and Cherokee families, especially mixed-bloods, often melted into the mountains and made their new homes in caves. The final three official detachments left Tennessee on September 20 and October 23. They arrived in the Cherokee Nation of Indian Territory on March 24, 1839, after littering the trail with the dead, nearly dead and important Cherokee artifacts.

Dr. Silas Scruggs Stacey recounted the story of his people, a story that was repeated many times in many families. His father, William Stacey, was reputed to be of Irish ancestors and his wife, Rebecca, a half-blood (often referred to as mixed-blood) Cherokee Indian, emigrated from Kentucky in 1838, in the company of his wife's people on the "Trail of Tears."

Little did William and his wife realize when they joined the Indian caravan at Hopkinsville, Kentucky, that their journey would be historically recorded in the annals of history. They crossed the Ohio near the mouth of the Cumberland and then passed through Southern Illinois to Cape Girardeau. By this time a severe winter had set in and delayed them from crossing the river because of the ice. Once across the river, they found it necessary to take the Northern route through central Missouri to Springfield. This route was necessary as the tribe that had preceded them on the Southern route to Fort Smith, had killed all the game upon which they had depended for subsistence.

It was mid-winter when the caravan arrived at Springfield. And it was here that William decided not to travel any farther with his wife's people. Instead they settled in what is now the Springfield area. They took shelter in a cave on the Finley River.

The cold winter and lack of game caused him to look for a more suitable location. It was not long before they found a tract of rich bottom land, surrounded by plenty of wild game for food, on Little Beaver Creek. Here they built a comfortable log cabin, cleared land, reared a large family and lived in peace and contentment for many years. As the years went by and they became too old to provide for themselves, their son, Dr. Silas Scruggs Stacey, moved them to Jasper in Newton County, Ark., where they lived to be very old. They are buried in unmarked graves in the Jasper Cemetery (Stacey Family History).

When the1998 vision of the spirit of murder being released again was given to me, I had been praying specifically over Forsyth, Rockaway Beach, and Merriam Woods. My research soon revealed that these towns were once native burial grounds.

In a report called, *ARCHEOLOGICAL AND HISTORICAL INVESTIGATIONS, OLD FORSYTH SITE, TANEY COUNTY, MO.*, the authors recorded the finds of a dig on Old Forsyth (now Shadowrock Park). Forsyth was built as a trading post over Indian burial grounds. “Further we know that the site was extensively used by prehistoric occupants of the region as witnessed by the abundance of prehistoric materials collected at the site. We have established that as early as 1806 the site was also associated with the settlement of removed Native American groups, primarily the Delaware, and that prior to 1827 a trading post was established at the confluence of Swan Creek and White River" (Bennett, Jr. and Blakely).

In an 1883 county newspaper, *Taney Enterprise*, a column appeared titled "Early Recollections and Reminiscences of Forsyth and Taney County, Number 9, J.H.M. wrote:

> Ask (Tom Layton) if he doesn't remember Mr. Snapp, and others, who once lived over and around there in those old by-gone days. There used to be an old graveyard across a little ravine above the house in the bottom at which a few were buried. (It is now known as Snapp's Cemetery, on the south side of the lake next to the bridge.) Wonder if it has been cared for? There was no graveyard on the town side then except one or two of Indians.

Elmo Ingenthron documented the Old Jennings cemetery on the property of early settler Jesse Jennings. The cemetery is referred to by old timers as the "old Cherokee cemetery" and was never relocated like the white settler's cemetery before 1913 when the Powersite Dam was completed. Quite possibly because Missouri Cook Casey held off Empire Electric officials with a shotgun refusing to sell the land for the lake until they met her price. They finally relented the day before Powersite Dam was completed. The next day, epic rainfall caused the entire reservoir to fill, and Missouri Cook Casey's land and subsequently the Old Jennings Cemetery were buried under the waters of Taneycomo. The Jesse Jennings farm began near the confluence of Bull Creek and White River and extended east toward McKinney Bend. Rockaway Beach is built upon this land.

It is true other Indian tribes were part of the Ozarks for brief periods of time but there were no lasting influences such as those left by the Osage and Cherokee. In addition, many early Taney County families can trace Cherokee ancestors in their bloodlines. That is why I have highlighted the tragedy of the Cherokee over the Creek, Chickasaw, Choctaw and Seminole who were also removed during this time frame.

By the 1850s, all Indian tribes had been resettled in Indian Territory and Missouri was void of any functioning tribe. However, several early settlers had taken Indian brides especially from the Cherokee because they integrated easily into white European society. Cherokee were one of the Five Civilized Tribes who had adopted many white cultural practices although they often firmly and privately held their religious rituals. Our land is sprinkled with these unique mixed-marriages and the clans they brought forth.

From these I came. My family's story is that of the mixed-bloods, those who were white enough to attempt to fight removal through the courts, but too dark to win against a government set on forced removal. My mother's people moved from western Kentucky in late 1838. They arrived January 1, 1839, at the Cherokee settlement on Huzzah Creek near Steelville, Missouri, and the Meramec River. My great-great-great grandfather, William Harrison Mathews, removed with his 76 year-old father, Peter Harrison Mathews, who had served the country during the Revolutionary War as a 13 year-old fifer. The two men came with their Cherokee wives, the 74 year-old Cherokee mother, several small children, along with a babe in arms who was my great-great grandfather, George Washington Mathews. Neither Peter's patriot status, nor my great-great grandfather's patriotic name could preserve Kentucky landholdings from the grasping hands of white settlers. Twenty years later, my great-great aunt and her family settled in the Blackwell Ferry area west of Kirbyville and south of Forsyth. My father's people, also mixed bloods, removed from western Tennessee into the Bootheel of Missouri settling in enclaves of what later became hard-working sharecroppers who tried to become white enough to survive.

On his birthday, December 11, 1890, John G. Burnett, who had been a 28 year old private in Captain Abraham McClellan's Company, 2nd Regiment, 2nd Brigade, Mounted Infantry, Cherokee Indian Removal, 1838-39, penned his life story and a first hand account of the Trail of Tears. In it Burnett wrote a prophetic indictment. "However, murder is murder whether committed by the villain skulking in the dark or by uniformed men stepping to the strains of martial music. Murder is murder and somebody must answer. Somebody must explain the streams of blood that flowed in the Indian country in the summer of 1838. Somebody must explain the 4,000 silent graves that mark the trail of the Cherokee's exile."

On Halloween weekend of 1998, at a conference hosted by Word of Faith Evangelist Billye Brim, Kenneth Copeland who is one-quarter Cherokee stood in proxy for Native Peoples as descendants of white settlers repented for their part in the Trail of Tears. This event took place at the southern most edge of Taney County and on the border of the Arkansas line on land formerly given by the government to the Cherokee in the 1817 Treaty of Turkey and revoked only a few decades later.

CHAPTER SIX

BIRTH OF A COUNTY

"Say unto the King and to the queen, humble yourselves, sit down! For your principalities SHALL COME DOWN, even the crown of your glory!" Jeremiah 13:18

Not only do principalities rule through people, but they are especially interested in establishing rule through governmental jurisdictions. In 1821 Missouri entered the Union as a slave state under the Missouri Compromise. This was a congressional agreement that regulated the extension of slavery in the United States for thirty years. Under the agreement, the territory of Missouri was admitted as a slave state, while the territory of Maine was admitted as a free state.

By 1818, the rapid growth in population in the North had left the Southern states, for the first time, with less than 45 percent of the seats in the U.S. House of Representatives. The U.S. Senate was evenly balanced between eleven slave and eleven free states. Therefore, Missouri's 1818 application for statehood, if approved, would give the slave states a majority in the Senate and reduce the Northern majority in the House. Henry Clay offered a "compromise." Missouri would be admitted as a slave state if Maine was admitted as a free state.

In 1821 Missouri complicated matters, however, by inserting a provision into its state constitution that prohibited free blacks and mulattoes from entering the state. Northern representatives objected to this language and refused to give final approval for statehood until it was removed. Clay then negotiated a second compromise that removed the offensive language from the Missouri constitution and substituted a provision that prohibited Missouri from discriminating against citizens from other states. Left unsettled was the question of who was a citizen.

Just one year before the tragedy of the Trail of Tears, the Missouri Legislature was busy carving a new county out of a huge piece of ground formerly called Greene County. The approximately lower one third of Missouri was hard to manage because it was an especially difficult section of land to traverse. Officials acknowledged this fact and began to carve out other counties. In 1837, Taney County consisted of roughly one thousand square miles of Ozarks hinterland and contained what is now known as Stone, Taney, Christian, Ozark and part of Douglas County. No white government had ruled over this region except that of the federal government until an official county government was formed and the first county seat was established. This was at the log home of Jesse Jennings at the mouth of Bull Creek, near what is the site of present day Rockaway Beach. Jesse Jennings was also the first census taker of the county and later went on to serve as State Representative. The Missouri Legislature named Taney County for Roger Brooke Taney, a Supreme Court Justice from Maryland. Taney later became the seated Chief Justice who rendered the Dred Scott Decision, the Supreme Court decision that became a flashpoint of the slavery debate.

Homesteading Begins

By the end of the 1830s, the government felt the "Indian issue" had been settled. The lands that once belonged to the Osage and then the Cherokee could now be legally inhabited by white settlers. Thousands of industrious Germans, lively Irish and sturdy Scots began to hack out lives in the land between the three rivers. Still, the land was sparsely settled until The Homestead Act of 1862. Signed into law in 1862 by Abraham Lincoln after the secession of southern states, this Act turned over vast amounts of the public domain to private citizens. 270 million acres or 10% of the area of the United States was claimed and settled under this act.

A homesteader had only to be the head of a household and at least 21 years of age to claim a 160 acre parcel of land. Settlers from all walks of life including newly arrived immigrants, farmers without land of their own from the East, single women and former slaves came to meet the challenge of "proving up" and keeping this "free land". Each homesteader had to live on the land, build a home, and make improvements and farm for 5 years before they were eligible to "prove up". A total filing fee of $18 was the only money required, but sacrifice and hard work exacted a different price from the hopeful settlers.

People interested in Homesteading first had to file their intentions at the nearest Land Office.

> A brief check for previous ownership claims was made for the plot of land in question, usually described by its survey coordinates. The prospective homesteader paid a filing fee of $10 to claim the land temporarily, as well as a $2 commission to the land agent. With application and receipt in hand, the homesteader then

> returned to the land to begin the process of building a home and farming the land, both requirements for "proving" up at the end of five years. When all requirements had been completed and the homesteader was ready to take legal possession, the homesteader found two neighbors or friends willing to vouch for the truth of his or her statements about the land's improvements and sign the "proof" document. After successful completion of this final form and payment of a $6 fee, the homesteader received the patent for the land, signed with the name of the current President of the United States. This paper was often proudly displayed on a cabin wall and represented the culmination of hard work and determination (National Park Service).

This significant legislation provided many wonderful opportunities for immigrant settlers, but in our region it also established the groundwork for a future conflict that would rip the fabric of our community to shreds under the cloak of justice.

Scots-Irish Settlers

In *Missouri's Tennessee Heritage*, Fred DeArmond wrote, "During the early decades of the 19th century the Tennessee settlers spread themselves all over the State of Missouri but later made their homes mainly in our Ozark highlands. Here they occupied almost solidly an area of 31,000 square miles.... and they still hold it."

The origins of these settlers trace back to King James I who, in 1607, was disturbed by reports of further turbulence in his unruly Irish dominion. He decided to act on a proposal by Sir Arthur Chichester, Lord Deputy of Ireland, to re-people the island with Protestants. That was the beginning of the Ulster Plantation. DeArmond wrote in *Scotch-Irish Heritage*, "The people were actually Protestants from Northern England and the Lowlands of Scotland. The proportion was roughly four Scots to one Englishman. They largely displaced the "aboriginal Irish" who were almost wholly Catholic. The Scots were Presbyterians and the English Anglicans were some dissenting creeds.

Therefore the early settlers who hailed from Ireland were many times descended from these transplanted Scotsmen and Englishmen. They often still held tightly to their superstitious and mystical spiritualisms in spite of the teachings of the Presbyterian Church. My husband and I are both descended from this stock.

During the years of research, I would often become confused. Mounds of notes, and piles of books would overwhelm me. How much of this was relevant to my quest to uncover the forces of the enemy? That was the cry of my heart June 19, 1999. Suddenly, I remembered a dream Steve (my husband) had recorded from the night of October 17, 1998:

> Gaye and I were in some sort of hospital, although it wasn't a regular hospital. She was sick, although she didn't act it. She was lying on a hospital bed and I was caring for her. A woman nurse came in and helped me make the bed. While looking around I found out that we were in an old motel. It was a nice one that had been named GALOWAY (odd spelling, I thought, but I saw the name on a brochure on the night stand.)

In the next scene, Gaye and I are on the deck of our house, not our present house but one similar. There was a lounge chair where Gaye was sleeping (still recovering from this sickness, I felt.) I heard several crows and saw something in a tree next to the deck. As I watched, I could see it was a wolf. When I first saw it, it seemed like a panther, which became a wolf. It seemed friendly. He was large and gray and walked out on a small limb to the end and continued on out into thin air. I tried to wake Gaye but she wouldn't awaken. The wolf looked us over, seemed to smile and then returned to the tree and disappeared. I finally woke Gaye and told her what had happened and she said the Lord had showed her the same thing in a vision while she was sleeping.

A crow then flew passed me and landed on the nearby picnic table. I caught it and held it with my hands encircling the body and wings. I walked over to the railing and beat the crow's head on the rail. It had tried to peck me but hadn't been able to. I struck it three or four times until it was dead. The other crows were going wild, but none would come close. I then threw the crow down to the ground.

Off the edge of the rail, I saw four or five odd looking animals walking upon the ground. They had different looking bodies and tails. One was like an anteater; another had a body like a fox or dog with its tail half skinned and half like a gray raccoon. I don't remember the others except one was a bird with a very, very long neck. There was neighbor behind us who raised exotic birds. And, another neighbor was having a yard sale. Then I woke up.

Of course, I knew in Steve's dream the strange animals and especially the wolf and crows pointed to witchcraft. I was interested in the name GALOWAY and why Steve had noted in his dream its particular spelling. According to the encyclopedia, Galoway, (now spelled Galloway,) or *Gallowa*, meaning "Land of the Foreign Gaels," is a peninsula-like region in southwestern Scotland. Gael is a name given to the Goidelic branch of the Celtic-speaking people who had originally come from the European continent and settled in Ireland. By A.D. 500, some Celtic-speaking people, whom Latin texts referred to as "Scotti," migrated northeast across the Irish Sea to this region where they established Celtic communities.

I was intrigued when I studied the map of the Galloway region especially when I realized one particular tip of this land seemed to point to a tiny isle off the southern coast whose name I quickly recognized—Isle of Man. Steve and I had just become aware of a law enforcement investigation concerning a powerful political figure in our community whom we knew to be tied to the occult. The investigation revealed criminal activities including a money trail woven in and out of nine other communities in the United States well- known for significant occult activity. Each money trail led to the Isle of Man. Certain financial loopholes available in the laws of the Isle offer opportunities to circumvent financial accountabilities that would otherwise be required by the United States government.

Isle of Man is a self-governing British Crown Dependency that traces its history from the rule of the Vikings to the Celtic traditions of A.D. 500. During the mid-thirteenth to early fifteenth centuries sovereignty passed frequently between Scotland and England. In 1765 the British Government purchased the entire island.

The political, cultural and religious life of the Islanders centers around a mound at St. John's thought to be a burial mound of the Bronze Age. There the Viking people offered their sacrifices. Relics which included the Viking God, Odin, have been discovered here. The same mound later became a Celtic religious site, and since that time has developed into a place where the tiny population of less than 30,000 people gathers for festivals and feasts.

I was urged to discover the clearly cultic religious traditions of the Celtics and Vikings who worshiped from the mound in the center of this island. These discoveries pointed me back to the Branson region and the Ozark Mountains.

"Among the ancient Celts, the druids were a class of priests and learned men. They formed an important part of every Celtic community in Ireland, Britain and Gaul and their leaders often rivaled kings and chiefs in prestige and power. They were judges, as well as priests and their counsel was eagerly sought by all classes of society.

The druids themselves avoided writing and preferred to pass along their tradition orally. However, some of the knowledge about druids was derived from Roman sources.

The druids were responsible for educating the sons of chiefs and generally served as the guardians of the sacred tradition.

The word druid itself seems to be related to the Celtic word for oak tree, "daur." Oak trees and mistletoe played an important part in druidic rituals as did human sacrifice. Victims were sacrificially burned in large wicker baskets in order to ensure military success or the health of the chief," (Scott Littleton, 1993).

Consider that demonic spirits which inspire such activity such as Celtic druidry as well as Viking paganism are still alive and at work influencing people today. In the chapter about the development of Branson, I will more feature more information on the Viking religion. When you read the chapter on the Bald Knobbers consider the Celtic druid's penchant for oak trees and human sacrifice.

Steve's dream had led me to Galloway which pointed me directly to the Isle of Man. It cannot be ignored that those who seek to harm our land and our people through the dark arts are financially connected to a land and people still inspired by these ancient demonic spirits. The beliefs they infect people with have been handed down from generation to generation opening wide the door for this same demonic activity.

During my research, I also uncovered an amazing relationship between druidry and Native American shamanism:

> *Working with animal powers is a central feature of shamanism. Many shamanic elements are woven into the philosophy and practice of druidry. Michael Harner, a world authority on shamanism, speaks of the shamanic way as one that is best defined as a method to open a door and enter a different reality. Much druid ceremony and meditation has as its goal journeying into other realties, and the word "druid" is related to words meaning both "oak" and "door"- with the symbol of the door or gateway being central in druidic teaching.
>
> Joseph Campbell, the great mythographer, has shown that there are a number of key

features that distinguish a shaman's art. These include: ritual dance, the possession of a wand or staff, ecstatic trance, the wearing of animal costume, identification with a bird, stag, or bull, becoming master of game animals and initiations and the control of a magical animal or familiar. Traces of possible ritual dances exist in the old folk dances, and there are numerous references to druid wands and staffs and ecstatic or altered states in the literature of druidry.

The remaining features listed by Campbell all relate to animals, and all are known to exist within the druid tradition. Druids were often identified as animals. They were called adders or piglets and they were said to possess, "crane, raven or bird knowledge". In summary, we can say that some elements of druidry are certainly shamanic, but druidry is not exclusively so- it also has alchemical, magical, and philosophical dimensions too" (The Druid Path).

We cannot ignore the fact that the occult exerted and still exerts influence on our region. Although this occultic influence will be more completely discussed in the chapter on witchcraft, let me say that what some consider naïve superstition may actually be occult powers at work. That is not to say all superstitions are cultic, however. Considering the early settlers and their frequent intermarriages with Cherokee, it is necessary to consider the influences on our people through native superstitions as well as dark magic.

A curious form of witchcraft which still lingers today existed among the early homesteaders. Ellen Gray

Massey recorded this form of witchcraft in her book, *Bittersweet Country*:

> Many natives of our land will be able to tell about their ancestor who was adept at water witching. Though some consider water witching to be mere superstition, others swear by the art. According to old timers, the witcher takes a forked branch and holds it tightly by the tongs, palms up, with the limb where the tongs meet sticking straight up in the air. As the water witcher walks across the ground, the limb twists toward the ground above or near a water supply. Water witching—or divining, as it is sometimes called has a long history. Stories often date back to the Middle Ages. Many Ozarkers have used this skill to figure out where to dig their well and the more skillful witchers are able to determine how deep beneath the earth's surface one would have to dig.

A friend of mine who descended from old settler families and who served in the mission field of Haiti for years once told me about the time they were set to drill a well in a remote village. The well driller was concerned because he had drilled several dry holes in the area and felt the village might prove to be another dry hole. The village elders brought their best water witchers who offered their services to the missionary.

The Holy Spirit rose up inside the missionary who responded, "The Lord will show us where the well should go. Witches will not!" He prayed and walked the village. At the direction of the Lord, he turned to the driller and pointed to a parcel of ground. "Drill here," he said. Reluctantly, the dubious driller set his equipment and began to drill. At one hundred feet, a pocket of the sweetest, coldest water in the region gushed to the surface. Fifteen years later, that well is still producing sweet water for the villagers.

I tell this story because the missionary involved could have relied on the “arts” known to his ancestors. However, the cloak over these “arts” must be ripped off because it will surely reveal an unholy reliance on supernatural powers other than God’s power. A true Believer in Jesus Christ must only rely on the power of God manifested in the person of the Holy Ghost. To do anything else hearkens back to pagan days, dark days, and days before the light of Jesus Christ was shined into our hearts.

Early homesteaders brought into our land cultural beliefs, often false and dangerous beliefs to which the undiscerning simply added Jesus Christ. In a similar way, the pagans of India today will simply add a crucifix to their collection of idols. But Jesus Christ did not come to be added to our collection of superstitions, occultic practices, and false beliefs. Jesus Christ comes to reign supreme over everything because He is supreme over everything.

CHAPTER SEVEN

OZARK SUPERSTITIONS

"The Hillman is secretive and sensitive beyond anything that the average city dweller can imagine, but he isn't simple. His mind moves in a tremendously involved system of signs and omens and esoteric auguries." Vance Randolph

In my first edition, I only brushed lightly on the superstitious beliefs found in the early Osage, Cherokee, and Ozarks culture. For one reason, I had not yet discovered Garrick Bailey's work concerning Osage religious practices. Another reason is that I was not as alarmed then as I am now about the superstitions that have crept into Charismatic and Pentecostal churches.

The "signs and wonders" movement, while initially appearing Biblically sound, in practice has too often deteriorated into superstition. Christian numerology, symbology, as well as colorology, have opened the door for some questionable beliefs to infiltrate the Body of Christ.

I believe there are true signs and wonders. However, I also believe the Church of today must cautiously sift through their experiences taking great care not to conclude every spiritual experience proves some sort of formulaic approach to God. The danger is, when all is said and done, humanity still wants to create its own way of figuring out (in order to control) God. It cannot be done.

Superstitions could also be called magical thinking. This is a term used to describe causal reasoning that looks for a correlation between acts or utterances and certain events. Magical thinking is prolific in many churches. I was surprised to be confronted by a magical thinking during a 1998 prophetic conference in Branson. The speaker talked about how every time she saw a red bird she hurried to "speak out." Her cry of "money cometh, money cometh, money cometh" was often rewarded with a check or unexpected offering in the mail that week.

Early folklorist Vance Randolph recorded several superstitions in his 1947 book entitled, *Ozark Superstitions*. The Cherokee and Osage both believed red birds portended good things. A Galena, Missouri woman was quoted as saying that children used to cry "money 'fore the week's out!" whenever they saw a redbird. The idea was that if you got it all said before the bird was out of sight, there would be money coming your way by the end of the week (Randolph).

There are a lot of red birds around our house, but I haven't noticed the accompanying wealth. On the other hand, I haven't "spoken out" about it either. I'm still stuck on the scripture in Deuteronomy 8:18 that says, "And you shall remember the LORD your God, for it is He who gives you power to get wealth, that He may establish His covenant which He swore to your fathers, as it is this day."

* Magical thinking and superstitions are irrational, changeable, and capable of being interpreted several different ways by different people groups. Superstitions may have a shred of truth, but they are not rooted and grounded in the Holy Scriptures, neither do they share a Biblical view of the character and nature of God. One day the Holy Spirit spoke to my heart, "Great care should be taken when trolling outside the realm of the written Word of God for spiritual revelation." My spirit rose up in

agreement, "We may tend to create our own version of God."

From the scriptures we can learn about many signs and wonders. The Children of Israel saw a host of them visited upon their Egyptian slave masters. Later, Moses smote a rock, and water came out. The sun stood still. The sun went backward. An ax head floated in the water. The dead were raised to life. The bones of a dead prophet caused a young man's body to come to life again. The widow's cruse of oil never emptied during a famine. Balaam's ass spoke. The three Hebrew children survived the fiery furnace.

Signs and wonders didn't end in the Old Testament days. When Jesus walked on the earth in bodily form, He changed water into wine. He walked on water. He took money from the mouth of a fish. He fed the multitudes with a few loaves and fishes. He cursed a fig tree, and it shriveled up. He told the storm to cease, and it became silent. At His word the dead were raised to life. Jesus did many signs and wonders.

The early Church saw many signs and wonders. Those bitten by poisonous snakes remained unharmed. Those imprisoned for the gospel's sake escaped unharmed. Those upon whom the shadow of Peter fell were made whole. God worked special miracles by the hands of Paul. Sicknesses and diseases departed and evil spirits went out of those who had handkerchiefs or aprons taken from his body and placed on them. Both Peter and Paul saw the dead raised to life.

God still does signs and wonders today. He still does special miracles today. He still heals. He still raises the dead. The Holy Spirit has provided for every believer the power by which these still take place.

However, it must be recognized that Satan can also perform lying signs and wonders. Not everything supernatural is of God. In 2 Thessalonians 2:8-11 Paul wrote, "And then shall that Wicked be revealed, whom the Lord shall consume with the spirit of His mouth, and shall destroy with the brightness of His coming: Even him, whose coming is after the working of Satan with all power and signs and lying wonders, and with all deceivableness of unrighteousness in them that perish; because they received not the love of the truth, that they might be saved. And for this cause God shall send them strong delusion, that they should believe a lie."

Our defense, our only protection against the onslaught of Satan's lying signs and wonders is to receive the love of the truth. Truth must be the banner that flies over every aspect of your life. You cannot live a lie and love the truth. You must speak the truth, read the truth, hear the truth, and love the truth. If you tell a lie, you will be lied to. You cannot sow a lie and reap the truth.

The original inhabitants of the Ozark Mountains were woefully short of Biblical truth and thus terribly open to superstitious beliefs. "Without knowledge my people perish," mourned Hosea. The Osage and other native tribes who followed as well as many of the early settlers, were without knowledge. They often died yoked to their native superstitions.

To the Osage, knowledge was the key to human survival (Bailey). Unfortunately they chose to glean their understanding of God from the cosmos. According to them, religious rituals could be done to aid in times of crisis and to effect changes. The priests carried the order of rituals, while the people observed the world around them and developed native superstitions.

Numbers were important. Four was the number of the cardinal points; north, south, east and west; thus, it was magical. Twenty-four was the number of the clan divisions, seven was the number of several religious rituals, three often represented the number of times certain chants or actions must be done. Thirteen was the number related to certain war rituals. Seven related to the seven stages or degrees of clan priesthood.

Colors had special meaning too. Red represented the recurrent day, black represented night or death. Osage blackened their faces before they went to war. You can image what they thought when they saw their first black slave.

The Osage had numerous important symbols. The golden eagle, black bear, puma, moon, great red boulder, the swan, the morning star (male star), the evening star (the female star), the crawfish, the spider, buffalo, rattlesnake, bull snake, spider, snapping turtle, mussel shell, deer, oaks, cedar, otter, willow tree, great crane, elderberry, nighthawk, flint corn, hailstones, the pipe, fire and much more could all be symbols used in religious rituals and were crammed with meaning.

Osage life was ruled by religious rituals so pervasive it is difficult to distinguish between what should be called their religion and what we would know as superstitions. However, according to Bailey, "Not all supernatural phenomena recognized by the Osages were integrated into their formal religion. They held other beliefs that might best be called 'folk beliefs'—including belief in prophets, were-animals, witchcraft, 'little people,' and ghosts."

Any new or strange whistling sounds were attributed to spirits or ghosts and created a feeling of fear. The French fur traders often sang songs, laughed and whistled. For some time this caused the Osage considerable concern for they could never be sure when a trader might start whistling (Ingenthron).

The Osage feared lightning and regarded it as a malicious act of the spirit realm. They would never use the wood from trees that had been struck by lightning as this would surely bring bad luck. Even the settlers who followed believed the same. Today, families in the Ozarks who still burn with wood shun a lightning blackened log.

The Cherokee called it thunderwood. During the Green Corn Ceremony the Cherokee used it within the sacred circle, where a deep pit would be dug and a branch of wood from a tree struck by lightning would be lit and used to bless the grounds for the ceremony. The coals from this thunderwood would be used to kindle the sacred fire in the pit in the center of the circle.

The Osage distinguished between true stories and fantasies and fables. Fables and myths were told only in the wintertime, when the snakes lie frozen underground. They are the guardians of the truth, and an untrue story arouses the anger of a snake (Bailey).The Osage believed that pointing at someone or something with their finger was likened to casting a spell or curse. If they wished to indicate something, they did so by looking at the object or person and pursing their lips as they slightly tossed their head toward it. They believed bees or birds and wild animals could communicate their misdeeds to Wah-Kon-Tah and were often accused of being tattletales.

They were deeply superstitious because they were deeply religious. In fact, of all the North American tribes, the Osage were considered the most deeply religious. For this reason, they believed breaking religious rituals and traditions often resulted in bad luck. Elaborate methods were developed by which a person could attempt to change his luck.

Crossing a stream or river could not be safely done without proper rituals and chants. An enemy could not be fought without the prerequisite ritualistic preparations. Anything unusual or new to them was met with superstition and was potentially the working of evil spirits or mischief makers.

When the Cherokee moved into the Ozark Mountains, they brought with them numerous superstitions. Certain numbers were important to them as well. Four represented the cardinal directions, although seven was the number of the sacred directions. North, south, east and west also included sun, earth and self. Seven represented the seven clans of the Cherokee. Seven also represented the height of purity and sacredness.

According to Cherokee David Vann, a directed descendent of Chief Joseph Vann, important colors were blue which represented peace and self reflection; white which represented corn, happy children and plentiful game; red which spoke of rebirth and new beginnings; black which represented death or the shadow life of the spirit; yellow spoke of the Creator, the Great Spirit; brown symbolized the earth and all her bounty; and green represented the dedication of the heart to purity and honesty (Vann).

Once again, religious beliefs and superstitions easily mingled. The cougar and the owl were the only ones who stayed awake for the seven nights of creation, thus they had a special regard. The cedar, pine, spruce, laurel and holly trees have leaves all year long. These plants also stayed awake and were given special powers (Vann).

Both Osage and Cherokee believed in moon signs as a method to decide when to plant or harvest, make war, embark on the hunt, or determine the nature of a newborn infant.

Cherokee superstitions included eating buzzard flesh to ward off disease. They believed its foul smell kept disease spirits at a distance. Sweat baths and bleeding were common practices for all sorts of things from preparing young men for the ball play to curing sickness.

Bleeding was the cure for rheumatism. Contained within the blood drawn out the shaman claimed to find a minute pebble or sharpened stick which he believed was placed in the body by an evil spell of an enemy. Snakebites were treated by rubbing the place of the bite in the opposite direction in which a snake coils because this is suppose to uncoil the poison from the body.

Both Cherokee and Osage medical practices were heavily sprinkled with superstition and religious ritual. If a patient died, either the person didn't properly believe or carry out the required rituals, or hadn't called the shaman or priest in enough time. Death was attributed to many causes, but never to the lack of proper medical care.

There were some cures affected because of the actual curative power inherent in certain plants. For example, the Cherokee knew long before the European settlers of the power of Goldenseal to act as a natural antihistamine. Hay fever, allergies and open wounds were and still are cured today by this plant. I use Echinacea-Goldenseal every spring and fall to alleviate seasonal allergies. It works for chronic sinus drainage too.

I do not however, administer the plant in conjunction with chants or ritualistic prayers. Honey was used as a natural antibiotic. It still is today. There is nothing wrong with using natural remedies that work. The problem is when superstitious actions must attend the use of natural remedies. That's a dangerous area where the potential for deception lies.

In 1818 Henry Rowe Schoolcraft referred to early settlers as having "burdensome superstitions" (Rafferty). It cannot be proven whether these issued forth from their ancestors or were beliefs assimilated by their close contact with the Osage and Cherokee. Suffice it to say superstition begets superstition.

Schoolcraft wrote, "Among all classes superstition is prevalent. Witchcraft and a belief in the sovereign virtue of certain metals so prevalent in those periods of the history of the progress of the human mind which reflects disgrace upon our species have still their advocates here." He wrote about a "hunter who was so convinced his rifle had been bewitched so that he could kill nothing with it and thus sold it on that account." The hunter suspected a malicious neighbor had laid a spell upon the rifle. Another hunter's wife was convinced her brass ring was an infallible remedy for the cramp, "which she was much troubled with before putting on the ring, but had not had the slightest return of it since" (Rafferty).

Vance Randolph wrote, "The Hillman is secretive and sensitive beyond anything that the average city dweller can imagine, but he isn't simple. His mind moves in a tremendously involved system of signs and omens and esoteric auguries. He has little interest in the mental procedure that the moderns call science, and his ways of arranging data and evaluating evidence are very different from those currently favored in the world beyond the hilltops. Ozark hill folks have often been described as the most superstitious people in America."

Most old people Randolph interviewed would scoff at the idea of being superstitious then tell for a "gospel truth" a strange and wild belief they personally held dear. Often these "gospel truths" conflicted from hill and vale depending on the clan of people interviewed.

Moon signs are a great example. Every Ozark resident was sure he knew when to plant spring potatoes in order to guarantee the best crop. March 17 was the tried and true date, unless you were from the family who knew it was "absolutely right" to plant in the light of the moon. Of course, other families scoffed at "them senseless superstitions" and planted each year in the dark of the moon.

The moon controlled a lot of the old settler's actions. Peering through the tree limbs to gaze upon a full moon was considered one way to "addle" your brain. On the other hand, the moon could help portend one's future mate. If a girl heard a dove and saw the new moon at the same instant, she had to repeat this verse:

"Bright moon, clear moon,
Bright and fair,
Lift up your right foot
There'll be a hair."

Then, she was to take off her right shoe and would naturally find in it a hair like that of her future husband (Randolph).

Physical characteristics have a lot to do with success, according to many early settlers. In both the Arkansas and Missouri Ozarks folks repeat the saying "a man with lots of hair on his legs is always a good hog raiser." I have a grown son with lots of hair on his legs, but he's never indicated a desire to raise hogs. However, his name in the Hebrew is translated as "wealthy," so we'll see how he does in the business community of computer programming.

A rainbow in the evening meant clear weather, but a rainbow in the morning indicated a storm within twenty-four hours. Hill folks watched and listened to their animals and chickens to learn if it was going to rain. "If a cock crows when he goes to bed, he'll get up with a wet head."

A rain on Monday, according to some meant that it would rain more or less every day that week. Others said if it rained on Monday there would be two or more rainy days, but that Friday would be bright and fair. However, if the sun "sets clear" on Tuesday, it was sure to rain before Friday (Randolph). Many native Ozarkers still believe rain during a funeral is a sign concerning the eternal destination of the dead person. "Blessed are the dead that the rain falls on," goes the saying.

Everybody who has lived here long enough knows that the answer concerning the plentitude of crops next growing season, can be found by cutting open a persimmon. If the little growth at the one end, between the two halves of the seed looks like a spoon, it means that everybody will raise bumper crops, but if the seed carries a tiny knife and fork instead, the growing season will be unsatisfactory.

Certain household items and accessories had distributive properties. Eggs carried in a man's hat would all hatch roosters. If a pregnant mother wished for a baby girl, she could place a frying pan underneath her mattress. Of course, she might carefully check her husband's side of the bed in which he could have hidden a jack-knife, a sure sign the baby was going to be a boy. Cherokee believed a leather sinew placed under the blankets held distributive properties and could make the unborn child tough and resilient.

It was and still is essential in some homes to eat black-eyed peas for dinner on New Year's Day for this seals the year for good luck. One granny woman knew that eating black eyed peas for New Year's dinner, coupled with wearing a pair of red garters and placing a dime under her plate, was a sure-fired way to garner good fortune for the entire year (Randolph).

Mountain medicine was practiced as carefully by settlers as by the Cherokee and the Osage before them. An abundance of native plants were harvested in order to create cures, potions, and spells and good luck charms. However, old timers often had a certain "way" of harvesting the plant or bark believing that it could make a vast difference in its effectiveness. Peach bark, for example, if gathered when the tree is shaved upward is supposed to prevent vomiting or stop diarrhea, but if the bark is shaved downward, the tea made from it is a violent purgative.

The Cherokee believed "dalani," literally "yellow," could be treated by rubbing the breast and abdomen of the patient with hands that had been rubbed together in a warm infusion of wild cherry bark. A song was sung and a prayer chanted. Old timers called the condition "biliousness" and believed it could also be cured by burning a saucer of whiskey while letting the blue flame toast a rancid bacon rind. The resulting juice was caught in the saucer. When the flame went out, the "witchified" potion was given to ease severe stomach pains.

Prayers and supplications were often intertwined with herbal cures. In the spring of 1934 a "prayin' corn doctor" visited Hollister, Missouri and treated many for corns and bunions by praying loudly over his herbal remedies. Another "yarb doctor" treated folks for kidney trouble with a poultice of green turnip tops that had been "blessed with the power of Christ Jesus" (Randolph). Both Osage priests and Cherokee shamans added vigorous prayers and chants to their remedies as well.

Old timers told of another type of healer different from the "yarb doctors." They made no pretense of using herbal remedies, but depended entirely on charms, spells, prayers, amulets, exorcisms and magic of one sort or another (Randolph). One chant to relieve the pain from superficial burns included the words:

One little Indian, two little Indians,

One named east, one named west,
The Son and the Father and the Holy Ghost,
In goes the frost, out comes the fire,
Ask it all in Jesus' name, Amen.

One old woman from Marshfield, Missouri, said that to stop bleeding you could repeat the sixth verse, sixteenth chapter of Ezekiel. Another woman from Seymour, Missouri, used the same verse, but added that "you have to call the person by name and the wound by name as you walk toward the sunrise repeating those verses." Randolph recorded that "perhaps the best blood stopper in McDonald County, Missouri, simply held up both hands and cried "Upon Christ's grave three roses bloom, stop, blood, stop!"

A Stone County, Missouri woman could supposedly cure goiters, boils, carbuncles, tumors, open sores, and even skin cancers by muttering some secret sayings adapted from the Bible. However, she told Randolph she wasn't allowed to tell anyone how it was done because she intended to pass the knowledge on to one of her own daughters before she died.

Rube Cummins of Day, Missouri, (just north of Branson) told Randolph he was adept at curing warts which he had done since he was a little boy. He said he just touched them and said "a little ceremony over them." When asked if the ceremony was something out of the Bible, he said emphatically that is was not (Randolph).

The body of a buzzard was somehow used by old timers to treat cancer, but it had to be done secretly because killing a buzzard meant seven years of crop failure for the whole countryside.

Intestinal worms could be killed by means of an old charm. Randolph found a woman at Noel, Missouri who told him "all you had to do was look the patient in the eye while crossing your fingers behind your back and repeat:

> God's mother Mary walked the land
> She held three worms in her hand,
> One white, one black, and t'other'n red,
> For Jesus' sake the worms are dead!"

The Cherokee chant to cure worms was a little more impressive. It began by declaring the disease was caused by a mere screech owl which the shaman at once banishes to the laurel thicket. In the rest of the chant, the doctor asserts that the trouble is caused by a mere hoot owl, a rabbit, or even "De'tsata," a malicious little dwarf who lives in caves in the river bluffs. These mischief makers are banished to their proper haunts.

James Mooney wrote in *Myths of the Cherokee*:

> Some shamans used an herb concoction which was blown upon the body of the suffering child just before the dark of night for four nights. He blew upon the back of the head, upon the left shoulder, right shoulder and finally upon the breast of the child as he or she was held in a sitting position facing the east. The child was not to be taken out of doors for four days lest a bird flying overhead fan the disease back into the body of the little one (Mooney).

Multiple births were viewed by old settlers as a sign of bad luck. Twins were always associated with tragedy and misfortune. On the other hand, both the Cherokee and the Osage viewed multiples as blessings. The Osage priests claimed twins for training in the priesthood.

Superstitions are probably as numberless as the humans who have ever lived and tried to "figure out" nature, the cosmos, heaven and God. Unfortunately, superstitions can become a form of idolatry because the person becomes fixated on the way things should be done rather than the "by whom" things are done. Superstitions are just another way Satan attempts to wrest Jesus Christ from the throne of a believer's mind, will, and emotions.

I recently viewed a video service from a major international ministry. During worship, one leader interrupted to tell the excited crowd that "three weeks ago we had a school of the Spirit where twelve people were healed by the Word of Knowledge and forty people were healed during the Holy Ghost Hokey Pokey." He went on to ask the worship leader to lead the congregation in the "Holy Ghost Hokey Pokey" and just "see what the Lord does." A groovy style of the old grade school song was sung while perhaps hundreds of believers joined him. The excitement was palatable as the leadership shouted, "power, power, healing, healing, healing, release miracles in Jesus' name." Later, people offered testimonies of healings in knees and backs, necks and elbows.

I steadfastly believe in the Holy Spirit gifting called Word of Knowledge and the healings the Holy Spirit does in Jesus' name, but I'm resistant to that being coupled with something called the "Holy Ghost Hokey Pokey." To do so, creates a dangerous opportunity for superstitions to develop, and the truth is, it is unnecessary to connect the two. The Lord was healing long before anyone invented the hokey pokey. If He tarries, He will be healing long after that silly song sinks into obscurity.

The truth that will keep us from strong delusions is that by chants, word-watching, magical thinking or speaking, or practicing any number of superstitions, we still cannot work our way to the blessings of health and wealth, safety and security, and ultimately eternal life. They are the gift of God.

CHAPTER EIGHT

BROTHER AGAINST BROTHER-THE UNCIVIL WAR

"My oldest brother and I were on opposite sides; he went into the Union army and I was Confederate." Uncle Joe McGill

While settlers in our region were hacking out a sparse living and attempting to tame the wild lands, a storm of unbelievable proportions was brewing between the North and the South. Suddenly, the Civil War was upon us and we would never be the same.

According to Elmo Ingenthron in *Borderland Rebellion*:

> In1860, the Taney County Census reported only 86 slaves and 24 slave-holding families. Five free slaves were also listed. Stone County had 16 slaves, and Christian County had 229 slaves. Poor white people settled most of the borderland with large families, seeking cheap land and needing few or no slaves. The topography and terrain of the region offered only a limited amount of virgin prairie soil and fertile bottomland where slavery would have been profitable in the production of cash crops. The average Ozarkian viewed slavery as being not

wholly good or totally bad, surely nothing so serious as to foment rebellion. In general, he was a loyal American (Ingenthron).

A confusing swirl of political yammering about slavery and states rights was occurring that appeared to have nothing to do with the Midwest. Then, Arkansas reconvened a convention on May 6, 1860 and voted for succession. Missouri was shocked and confused. To be loyal to the Union would mean disloyalty to their relatives in Arkansas. Families and communities were ripped apart.

In a 1915 booklet by E. J. Hoenshel entitled *Stories of the Pioneers*, Uncle Joe McGill was quoted as saying, "I was fifteen in August after the war broke out, just a boy. People were about equally divided here and families were divided too. Father and sons were often on opposite sides and brother fought against brother. My oldest brother and I were on opposite sides; he went into the Union army and I was Confederate."

Captain James Van Zandt, a Methodist Minister from Kirbyville remembered, "I went into the Union army in 1861 in Company K, 24th Missouri Infantry. I organized the first company of Union soldiers that went out from Springfield. Lots of my friends went into the Southern army, but I said I had fought for this nation in one war, and I couldn't go back on her now. We talked about what we should do if we should meet in battle on different sides during the war, and I said, 'Boys, if I meet you in battle, I'll shoot you if I can, but if I take any of you prisoners, I'll treat you like my own children'"(Hoenshel).

"The heartaches, mental anguish, physical pain, torture and endless distress suffered by women in the border struggle were often beyond description then and are difficult to comprehend from this distant view. There were reports of women being tortured by the enemy in efforts to obtain information. As the war continued, mothers shepherding starving, half-clad families were forced to flee the border zone. Almost daily, refugees flowed northward or southward. Some followed the dictates of their loyalties. To many it was not a matter of loyalty so much as it was the last hope of survival for themselves and their children" (Ingenthron).

Lt. C.W. Huff, stationed with the Union troops at Forsyth, wrote in his diary:

> March 6, 1863: A couple of families from Searcy County Arkansas came in today, but the bushwhackers had overhauled them and taken from them whatever they wished and then allowed them to proceed. I never saw such families of children as they bring with them. None of them have less than six and number as high as fifteen. Those who came in today are certainly objects of charity and on such a day as this, they come to us muddy, wet to the skin and nearly frozen.
>
> March 18, 1863: A large number of women with their children came to our camp today with various stories concerning their husbands being forced to flee their homes to escape being conscripted into the Rebel army or that they have enlisted in Arkansas Union regiments and being destitute at home and persecuted by their neighbors have sought our lines for protection and provisions, and many of them expecting to meet relations here. One house in this place has been given to them. I think there are not less than a couple of dozen women here and not less

than a hundred children from ages of one week to 14 years.

In regards to this anguish, the Church for the most part remained passive. Ingenthron commented:

> Christianity should have been a potent force that bound people together in brotherly love and aided them in resolving their differences. United, the churchmen might have had great influence in preventing the war or in mitigating the anguish and suffering associated with it. Instead of grasping their great opportunity for solving the problems, all too often churchmen became a part of them. The warriors in the army of the Lord, who had been called to fight the evils of mankind, appear to have divided their forces to do battle with each other, forgetting the Christian principles mandated by the Holy Bible. On one occasion when a prominent church member was making a speech filled with hatred for the enemy, a bystander asked what had become of the Biblical injunction to love one's enemies. The speaker replied that this was a different kind of an enemy than those referred to in the Bible."

In *Our Religious Heritage,* Earl T. Sechler wrote, "(The) center of anti-union feeling was said to have been in the members of the Christian Church (Disciples of Christ) where slaveholding Revs. Carleton and Joel H. Haden were prominent preachers. Founders of the denomination, Thomas and Alexander Campbell had blessed the institution of slavery with no less than 17 biblical texts."

Colonel Monks mentioned the churchmen in his published memoirs:

> About one-tenth of the Rebel officers appeared to be Baptist and Methodist preachers, and frequently when they would go into camp would call a large number of the men together and very often take the prisoners and place them nearby, under heavy guard, and then convene religious services. They always took for a text some subject in the Bible and the author well remembers the taking of subjects on the book of Joshua where Joshua was commanded to pass around the fortification of the enemy and blow the ram's horn and the fortifications fell, and the God of Joshua was the same God that existed today and there was no question but that God was on the side of the South and all they had to do was to have faith and move on, attack the lop-eared Dutch (Germans) and God was sure to deliver them into their hands.

God's people made the classic mistake of interpreting the Word of God through the monocles of popular cultural beliefs instead of the character and nature of God. God's nature never has been nor ever will it be the nature of oppression proved by the fact He sent His only Son to set the oppressed free. The Church in the Ozark Mountain region was blinded to the fact their God is color blind. This blindness came at a high price for especially those caught in the crossfire of an unnecessary conflict.

Two major Civil War battles took place in our region: the Battle of Wilson's Creek and the Battle of Pea Ridge. Here are synopses of both of them taken from information presented at each historic battlefield:

BATTLE OF WILSON'S CREEK (The Battle of Oak Hills) (Near Present day Springfield, Missouri)
August 10, 1861
Union Commander Brigadier General Nathaniel Lyon
Rebels Commander General Sterling Price and General William McCullough
Union Troops- 5,400
Rebels-11,000

Plan of attack-surprise
Col. Sigel flanked rebels to the southwest by cutting off their retreat by the Fayetteville Road.

Fatal error- Col. Sigel (Union) mistook the gray uniformed Louisiana troops for the Union Iowa Grays and did not halt their advance until too late.

Union lost all but two commanders; Major Sturgis and Col. Sigel
Casualties
Union- 1,091 killed, wounded or missing
Rebels-1,245 killed, wounded or missing
Battle time- 5 hours

PEA RIDGE CAMPAIGN (The Battle of Elk Horn Tavern) (Near present day Bentonville, Arkansas)
March 6-8, 1862
Union Commanders- General Curtis and General Sigel
Rebel Commanders- Generals Price, McCullough, Van Dorn and Albert Pike

General Pike's command included 3,600 Indians, mostly Cherokee
General Pike rode in a carriage driven by his Negro body servant, Brutus, and was accompanied by John Ross, Principal Chief of the Cherokee Indians.
Union Troops- 10,500 cavalry and infantry and 49 pieces of artillery
Rebel Troops- 14,000 men and 50 pieces of artillery

Fatal error- Pike's Indians terrorized Sigel's men. Sigel's men fled. Too soon the Indians stopped to gather the spoils. Union Col. Osterhaus turned artillery on Indians. Panicked Indians fled. Rebels retreated.

Casualties
Union- 1,351 killed, wounded or missing
Rebels- 800-1,000 killed and wounded, 200-300 captured

War atrocities were common and often honored during this gruesome chapter in our nation's history. After a particularly bloody battle at Pea Ridge, captured soldiers were ordered taken to the Union headquarters in Springfield, MO. One hundred captives never arrived. Today, Stone County elders note a pond (located where the Wal-Mart Supercenter in Branson West is now) into which "more than 100 rebel soldiers were dumped after they were executed on the march from Pea Ridge to Springfield, MO."

On July 22, 1861, a minor but still fierce battle took place in Forsyth, MO. Rebel forces had seized early on the county seat of Forsyth. Forsyth was receiving supplies shipped up the White River at the order of General Price. Union command in Springfield chose General Sweeny with his 1,200 men to raid Forsyth and cut off supplies. The Rebels numbered about 150 men.

Union troops destroyed the courthouse in the shelling. Five rebels were killed, three were taken prisoner and the rest escaped back to their homes. As soon as the Federals withdrew, the Confederates crept back to the courthouse and raised the Rebel flag, (Ingenthron).

Fall of 1998

While in intercession at the altar, the Lord showed me a vision of a large river. I was viewing it from a great distance when I detected lots of flashing silver streaks and movement upon the surface of the river. In the vision, I drew closer until I could see that the flashes of silver were the bodies of fish. There were so many fish jammed into the river that they were coming to the top and were clearly visible. I could have grabbed them by the handsful.

I asked the Lord the meaning of this and He said, "Just as the White River was filled with fish because it was not regularly fished by the men during the Civil War, so is my river, filled with souls, waiting to be caught. But just as the Civil War, brother against brother, countryman against countryman, kept the men from fishing the river, so has the civil war in the Church kept my men from bringing in the souls. As soon as the Civil War is over, the harvesting can begin."

Later in my research, I found this story:

> When I lived near Father, we would often go down the river to fish. It was no trouble to get fish anytime you wanted them. The bottom of the river was covered with them. The fall after peace was made people came in from the north, wagon after wagon for fish. Of course, at that time they were allowed to seine all they wanted

to. I saw seven thousand pounds seined out at one draw. This was about three miles below where my farm is now. There were so many fish in the seine we could not draw it out. We carried out fish and piled them on the gravel bar till we had a pile six feet high. The fish weighed from two to forty pounds. The seine was stretched up and down the river 70 or 80 yards, and there were so many fish in it we couldn't get the "bag" of the seine nearer the bank than thirty yards. I know this sounds a little "fishy", but ask Uncle Prather McQuerter—he was there too. (Hoenshel)

CHAPTER NINE

TIME FOR DECEPTION

"Some of the symbols are displayed there to the initiate, but he is intentionally misled by false interpretations. It is not intended that he shall understand them; but it is intended that he shall imagine that he understands them."
Albert Pike

Much of my research has been guided by dreams and visions and divine appointments. Such was the case in 1999 when I undertook an innocent trip to Wal-Mart. In route, I carelessly flipped on the local radio station and was transfixed by a man named Ron Carlson revealing the awful truth behind Freemasonry. I listened to the entire program then ordered the accompanying video tape with a great deal of trepidation.

At that time, my mother was the private duty nurse for one of the most prominent men of our community, Dr. M. Graham Clark, the founding President of the college program of the School of the Ozarks (now College of the Ozarks). He was a community leader, a Rotarian, an ordained Presbyterian minister and a 33rd degree Mason.

Dr. Clark watched the videotape, *Freemasonry, From Darkness to Light?* by Jeremiah Films and hosted by Ron Carlson. In it, former Masons as high as 32nd degrees, confessed the secrets of Freemasonry and its intentional deception of members. Dr. Clark was very upset by the video. He argued that the information was inaccurate and untrue. I was confused. I had felt like my finding this information and uncovering the Masonic roots of our region was divinely appointed by God and an important part of the spiritual history research. Dr. Clark denied the contents of the videotape and then told me he even had one of the books quoted in the tape. He offered to let me look at the book, but we could never find it.

One day Dr. Clark gave my mom permission to go through one of his storage buildings and select old books (which Mom dearly loves). I offered to go with her and help her move the heavy boxes. After hours in the dusty storage building, we decided to leave when I pulled out one last box. It was full of family yearbooks and scrapbooks. Then my eye fell on a very large volume at the bottom of the box. It was the book we had looked for months earlier.

For those who do not believe masonry is a clever, satanic deception of witchcraft ceremonies, they are welcome to read pages copied directly from the *Encyclopedia of Freemasonry,* written in 1917 by Albert G. Mackey, a 33rd degree mason and one of the foremost Masonic leaders.

In our region Freemasonry was positioned to have a significant influence. The bloody Civil War chapter was closed and our people were quickly settling down to the work of making a living for their families by hacking out cropland in this rocky terrain. Mankind has always been drawn to the idea of elite groups and fellowships. The people of our region were no different. They were perhaps particularly ripe to the idea of secret societies because our first people, the Osage, were too.

One of the four prominent features of the Osage Indians was secret societies, a part of their tribal governing system and their religious system. Out of these roots grow Masons of Taney County. On July 8, 1872, Forsyth Lodge No. 453, A.F. and A.M. were officially established. In the early days the Lodge held festivals celebrating Saint John the Baptist and Saint John the Evangelist days. Saint John the Baptist day fell on or near the first day of summer and Saint John the Evangelist day on or near the first day of winter. In occult terms, those are the summer and winter solstices, respectively.

Old timers in Masonry will remember that all across Missouri the Masons and other Lodges often occupied the second story of some building. First of all, it usually offered cheaper rent options and secondly, they need not close the windows on hot summer evenings to prevent the "uninitiated" from hearing their secret practices.

In December of 1884, before the Bald Knobbers came into being, a lot was purchased and a contract let for the foundation of the Masonic lodge. The two-story building stood at the northeast corner of Benton and Lincoln streets in Forsyth. When Bull Shoals Lake was formed, this building was moved to the present site of Forsyth high atop the hill. In 2001, Spirit-filled Christians became owners of the building unaware of its history. A Spirit-filled believer moved her beauty shop into the building, as a tenant. In February, old and faulty wiring ignited a blaze in the attic that soon consumed and destroyed the entire building.

In 1889 the lodge at Protem was formed. In 1900 the lodge at Kirbyville was established, and Branson's lodge was created in September of 1907.

When the School of the Ozarks (now College of the Ozarks) was begun in Forsyth, the lodge voted to provide the cornerstone and dedicate it. It was laid on October 17, 1906 with appropriate ceremonies. After fire destroyed the School and the new school was built near Hollister, the cornerstone was planted in the step of the Masonic lodge at Forsyth. In 1951, the lodge members decided to return the cornerstone to the School of the Ozarks where a member of the faculty and fellow member, Brother Wright, assured members it would be treasured. It now stands on a pedestal in the Ralph Foster Museum on the college campus.

In Branson, Masons were busy laying cornerstones "with appropriate ceremonies." According to Albers and Stacey, in their book, *Hometown Branson:*

> An impressive ceremony was conducted on August 31, 1922 to lay the cornerstone of the new Branson High School. The PTA, the American Legion and the Missouri Masonic Grand Lodge led the march from the business district to the new building. Business houses closed for the event and a large crowd watched as a polished marble slab was placed and judgment of its workmanship passed upon by Master Masons. First with a square standing morally for virtue, but used by operative masons to square their work; second a level, symbol of equality used to lay horizontals, third a plumb for uprightness and rectitude of conduct used to raise perpendiculars. Next an offering of corn was poured over the surface for virtue, wisdom and gratitude; a measure of wine for joy and plenty blessings and prosperity to our nation; and lastly, oil for peace.

One of the reasons Freemasonry has deceived so many is that although it is a system of complex beliefs, few members rise to the levels of achievement necessary to have these beliefs shared with them.

Masonry is, according to its own philosophers, a system of pure religion expressed in symbols, one that cannot be understood without knowledge of the true meaning of them. This makes a proper understanding of those symbols terribly important. For the "Christian Mason," accepting and guarding those symbols and their "secrets" with his physical life at stake, is his highest goal. Masonry is characterized by blood oaths. In the Apprentice or First Degree, the initiate confesses, "...binding myself under no less penalty than that of having my throat cut across, my tongue torn out by its roots, and my body buried in the rough sands of the sea at low-water mark." The Master Mason swears "...under no less penalty than that of having my body severed in two, my bowels taken from thence and burned to ashes, the ashes scattered before the four winds of heaven."

Masons take a bizarre communion in which the unfortunate deceived confess:

> What is to us the chief symbol of man's ultimate redemption and regeneration? Answer: In the bread we eat and the wine we drink tonight may we enter into and from us part the identical particles of matter that once formed the material bodies called Moses, Confucius, Plato, Socrates and Jesus of Nazareth. In the truest sense, we eat and drink the bodies of the dead; and cannot say that there is a single atom of our blood or body, the ownership of which some other soul might not dispute with us.

Symbols proliferate this belief system. The correct understanding of these symbols is the key (they believe) to their eternal destiny. They are trusting in the teachings of the Lodge concerning these symbols with their eternal redemption, or damnation, at stake. Herein lays the most terrible manifestation of Masonic morality, that philosophy of the elite, which makes whatever they do "right" because it is they (the elite) who do it. Having established and taught the sincere but deceived masses of Masons (the Blue Lodge Masons) that everything depends upon their proper understanding of the symbols of Masonry, they have then deliberately deceived them as to the true meaning of those symbols. Hear the arrogant words of Albert Pike, Supreme Pontiff of Universal Freemasonry, that preeminent Masonic authority who authored, *Morals and Dogma*:

> The Blue Degrees are but the court or portico (porch) of the Temple. Some of the symbols are displayed there to the initiate, but he is intentionally misled by false interpretations. It is not intended that he shall understand them; but it is intended that he shall imagine that he understands them... their true explication (explanation and understanding) is reserved for the Adepts, the Princes of Masonry (those of the 32nd and 33rd Degrees).

Since the true meaning of Masonic symbols (and thus, the true meaning of Masonry itself) is to be known only by the Prince Adepts of Masonry, let us consider what they say concerning them. Albert Pike, Albert Mackey, J. D. Buck, Daniel Sickles and others teach that Masonry is a revival of the Ancient Mysteries (the mystery religions of Babylon, Egypt, Persia, Rome and Greece).

These Ancient religions had two meanings or interpretations. One was the apparent (exoteric) meaning known to the uninitiated, ignorant masses; the other (esoteric) meaning was the true meaning, entirely different, known only to a small, elite group initiated into their secrets and secret rituals of worship. These mystery religions were forms of nature-worship, more specifically and most commonly the worship of the sun as source and giver of life to the earth. Since ancient times, this worship of the sun (and of the moon, stars and of nature in general) has been sexual in its out workings and rituals. Since the sun's rays, penetrating the earth and bringing about new life, have been central to such worship, the phallus, the male 'generative principle,' has been worshipped and the rituals climaxed with sexual union in the mystery religions of Isis and Osiris, Tammuz, Baal, etc. Since the Ancient Mysteries (especially those of Egypt) are in fact the Old Religion of which Freemasonry is a revival, the symbols of Masonry should be expected to be phallic in true meaning. This, in very fact, is the case. The following will suffice to illustrate this astonishing fact.

The Square and Compass

Blue Lodge Masons are taught that the Square is to remind them that they must be "square" in their dealings with all men, i.e., to be honest. The Compass, they are taught, is to teach them to "circumscribe their passions," i.e. to control their desires and to be temperate. The real meaning of these "great lights," however, is sexual. The Square represents the female (passive) generative principle, the earth, and the baser, sensual nature; and the Compass represents the male (active) generative principle, the sun/heavens, and the higher, spiritual nature. The Compass, arranged above the Square, symbolizes the (male) Sun impregnating the passive (female) Earth with its life-producing rays. The true meaning then is two-fold: the earthly (human) representations are of the man and his phallus, and the woman with her receptive cteis (vagina). The cosmic meaning is that of the active Sun (deity, the Sun-god) from above, imparting life into the passive Earth, (deity, the earth/fertility goddess) below and producing new life.

The Letter "G"

The Blue Lodge Mason is taught that the "G" in the Masonic symbol represents God. Later on, he is told that it also represents "deity." Later still, he is told that it represents "geometry." In reality, this letter represents the "generative principle," the Sun-god and, thus, the worshipped phallus, the male "generative principle..." In its position (along with the Square and Compass) on the east wall over the chair (throne) of the Worshipful Master, it is the representation of the Sun, thus of the Sun-god, Osiris. Its earthly meaning, then, is of the sacred phallus; its cosmic meaning is of the Sun, worshipped since antiquity by pagans while facing the East. (Remember the arrangement of the Osages “temple”?)

The Vertical Lines

The two vertical lines touching the sides of the circle are represented to the Blue Lodge Mason as "the Holy Saints John." By this is meant John the Baptist and John the Apostle. In reality, the two vertical lines represent the summer and winter solstices, the shortest and longest nights of the year, respectively. These nights are, and have been since antiquity, important periods for pagan worship. Concerning these two lines, Albert Mackey has written ("Symbolism of Freemasonry," page 352), "The lines touching the circle in the symbol of the point within a circle are said to represent St. John the Baptist and St. John the Evangelist, but they really refer to the solstitial points, Cancer and Capricorn, in the Zodiac."

The Bible

The Bible, only one of the "Three Great Lights" of Masonry (along with the Square and Compass), is represented to Blue Lodge Masons as symbolizing truth. In reality, the Bible may be replaced with the Koran, the Book of the Law, The Hindu scriptures or any other "holy book" depending on the preferences of the men in the Lodge. In most American Lodges, the members are told that all the Masonic system and its rituals are "based on the Bible." Such however is not the case. In Chase's "Digest of Masonic Law," pages 207-209, it is clearly written that "Masonry has nothing whatever to do with the Bible" and that "it is not founded upon the Bible for if it were it would not be Masonry; it would be something else."

In *Morals and Dogma*, Albert Pike wrote, “Masonry is a search after light. That search leads us directly back, as you see, to the Kabalah.” The Kabalah, then, seems to be the actual sourcebook of Masonry and the Bible is instead merely (as it is spoken of in the ritual) a piece of the "furniture" of the Lodge.

Pike was the Sovereign Grand Commander of the Masons from 1858 until his death in 1891. He was a repulsive man. Weighing over 300 pounds, he was often found sitting naked astride a phallic throne in the woods. He surrounded himself by a band of prostitutes and wagon loads of food and alcohol which he would consume over the course of a few days until he passed into a stupor. Pike lived for a time in Oklahoma among the Cherokee Indians. Later, he led Cherokee warriors in the Battle of Pea Ridge (Arkansas) where they were defeated. After the Civil War, Pike moved to Arkansas and was a well known practitioner of Satanism. Portraits of his later years show him wearing the symbol of Baphomet around his neck. He is credited with developing the belief systems of Modern Freemasonry. Unfortunately, he is memorialized by statues in his honor in Little Rock and by the Albert Pike Highway which runs from Hot Springs, Arkansas, to Colorado Springs, Colorado.

Well-indoctrinated Masons commonly reject information that proves the intricate deception in which they have been involved. In fact, you might be surprised to know whose names appear on the membership rolls of local Masonic Lodges. Business leaders, pastors, political leaders and retirees have been transfixed by this elaborate deception. In fact, a prominent monument to a well-known business person, a 33rd degree honorary mason, was erected on the east side of the gas station at the intersection of U.S. 65 Highway and Missouri 248 Highway. For those who believe I have manipulated information to "make Masons look bad," view for yourself actual pages from Albert Mackey's *Encyclopedia of Freemasonry.* Mackey is considered by Masons to be the second great authority on this subject.

TSCHOUDY
950
TRUE

Truth. The real object of Freemasonry, in a philosophical and religious sense, is the search for truth. This truth is, therefore, symbolized by the WORD. From the first entrance of the Apprentice into the Lodge, until his reception of the highest degree, this search is continued. It is not always found, and a substitute must sometimes be provided. Yet whatever be the labors he may perform, whatever the ceremonies through which he may pass, whatever the symbols in which he may be instructed, whatever the reward he may obtain, the true end of all is the attainment of truth. This idea of truth is not the same as that expressed in the lecture of the first degree, where Brotherly Love, Relief, and Truth are there said to be the "three great tenets of a Mason's profession." In that connection, truth, which is called a "divine attribute, the foundation of every virtue," is synonymous with sincerity, honesty of expression, and plain dealing. The higher idea of truth which pervades the whole Masonic system, and which is symbolized by the WORD, is that which is properly expressed to a knowledge of God.

DRUIDICAL
257
OR A ES EKE

Druidical Mysteries. The Druids were a sacred order of priests who existed in Britain and Gaul, but whose mystical rites were practised in most perfection in the former country, •where the isle of Anglesea was considered as their principal seat. Hig-gins thinks that they were also found in Germany, but against this opinion we have the positive statement of Caesar.

The meanings given to the word have been very numerous, and most of them wholly untenable. The Romans, seeing that they worshipped in groves of oak, because that tree was peculiarly sacred among them, derived their name from the Greek word, *Zpvs, drus;* thus absurdly seeking the etymology of a word of an older language i'n one comparatively modern. Their derivation would have been more reasonable had they known that in Sanscrit *druma* is an oak, from *dru,* wood. It has also been traced to the Hebrew with equal incorrectness, for the Druids were not of the Semitic race. Its derivation is rather to be sought in the Celtic language. The Gaelic word *Druiah* signifies a holy or wise man; in a bad sense, a magician; and this we may readily trace to the Aryan *druh,* applied to the spirit of night or darkness, whence we have the Zend *dru,* a magician. Druid-ism was a mystical profession, and in the olden time, mystery and magic were always confounded. Vallencey *(Coll. Reb. Hib.,* iii. 503,) says: "Welch, *Drud,* a Druid, *i. e.* the absolver or remitter of sins; so the Irish *Drui,* a Druid, most certainly is from the Persic *dv.ru,* a good and holy man;" and Ousely *(Coll. Orient.,* jv. 302,) adds to this the Arabic *dari,* which means a wise man. Bosworth *(A. S. Diet.)* gives *dry,* pronounced *dru,* as the Anglo-Saxon for "a magician, sorcerer, druid." I think that with the old Celts the Druids occupied the same place as the *Magi* did with the old Persians.

Druidism was divided into three orders or degrees, which were, beginning with the lowest, the *Bards,* the *Prophets,* and the *Druids.* Higgins thinks that the prophets were the lowest order, but he admits that it is not generally allowed. The constitution of the Order was in many respects like that of the Freemasons. In every country there was an Arch-Druid in whom all authority was placed. In Britain it is said that there were under him three arch-flamens or priests, and twenty-five flamens. There was an annual assembly for the administration of justice and the making of laws, and, besides, four quarterly meetings, which took place on the days when the sun reached his equinoctial and solstitial points. The latter two would very nearly correspond at this time with the festivals of St. John the Baptist and St. John the Evangelist. It was not lawful to commit their ceremonies or doctrines to writing, and Caesar says *(Bell. Gall.,* vi. 13.) that they used the Greek letters, which was, of course, as a cipher, but Higgins (p. 90) says that one of the Irish Ogum alphabets, which Toland calls *secret writing,* "was the original, sacred, and secret character of the Druids."

The places of worship, which were also places of initiation, were of various forms: circular, because a circle was an emblem of the universe; or oval, in allusion to the mundane egg, from which, according to the Egyptians, our first parents issued; or serpentine, because a serpent was a symbol of Hu, the druidical Noah; or winged, to represent the motion of the Divine Spirit; or cruciform, because a cross was the emblem of regeneration. Their only covering was the *clouded canopy,* because they deemed it absurd to confine the Omnipotent beneath a roof; and they were constructed of embankments of earth, and of unhewn stones, *unpolluted with a metal tool.* Nor was any one permitted to enter their sacred retreats, unless *he bore a chain.*

The ceremony of initiation into the Druidical Mysteries required much preliminary mental preparation and physical purification. The aspirant was clothed with the three sacred colors, white, blue, and green; white as the symbol of Light, blue of Truth, and green of Hope. When the rites of initiation were passed, the tri-colored robe was changed for one of green; in the second degree, the candidate was clothed in blue; and having surmounted all the dangers of the third, and arrived at the summit of perfection, he received the red tiara and flowing mantle of purest white. The ceremonies were numerous, the physical proofs painful, and the mental trials appalling. They commenced in the first degree, with placing the aspirant in the pastes, bed or coffin, where his symbolical death was represented, and they terminated in the third, by his regeneration or restoration to life from the womb of the giantess Ceridwin, and the commital of the body of the *newly born* to the waves in a small boat, symbolical of the ark. The result was, generally, that he succeeded in reaching a safe landing-place, but if his arm was weak, or his heart failed, death was almost an inevitable consequence. If he refused the trial through timidity, he was contemptuously rejected, and declared forever ineligible to participate in the sacred rites. But if he undertook it and succeeded, he was joyously invested with all the privileges of Druidism.

The doctrines of the Druids were the same as those entertained by Pythagoras. They taught the existence of one Supreme Being; a future state of rewards and punishments; the immortality of the soul, and a metempsychosis; and the object of their mystic rites was to communicate these doctrines in symbolic language, an object, and a method common alike to Druidism, to the Ancient Mysteries and to Modern Freemasonry.

Druses. A sect of mystic religionists who inhabit Mounts Lebanon and Anti-Lebanon, in Syria. They settled there about the tenth century, and are said to be a mixture of Cuthites or Kurds, Mardi Arabs, and possibly of Crusaders; all of whom were added, by subsequent immigrations, to the original stock to constitute the present or modern race of Druses. Their religion is a heretical compound of Judaism, Christianity, and Mohammedism; the last of which, greatly modified, predominates in their faith. They have a regular order of priesthood, the office being filled by persons consecrated for the purpose, comprising principally the emirs and sheiks, who form a secret organization divided into several degrees, keep the sacred books, and hold secret religious assemblies. Their sacred books are written in antiquated Arabic. The Druses are divided into three classes or degrees, according to religious distinctions. To enable one Druse to recognize another, a system of passwords is adopted, without an interchange of which no communication is made that may give an idea of their religious tenets. (Tien's *Druse Religion Unveiled.)*

Dr. Clarke tells us in his *Travels* that "one class of the Druses are to the rest what the initiated are to the profane, and are called Okkals, which means spiritualists; and they consider themselves superior to their countrymen. They have various degrees of initiation."

Col. Churchill, in his *Ten Years' Residence on Mount Lebanon,* tells us that among- this singular people there is an order having many similar customs to the Freemasons. It requires a twelve months' probation previous to the admission of a member. Both sexes are admissible. In the second year the novice assumes the distinguishing mark of the white turban, and afterwards, by degrees, is allowed to participate in the whole of the mysteries. Simplicity of attire, self-denial, temperance, and irreproachable moral conduct are essential to admission to the order.

All of these facts have led to the theory,—based, however, I think, on insufficient grounds,—that the Druses are an offshoot from the early Freemasons, and that their connection with the latter is derived from the Crusaders, who, according to the same theory, are supposed to have acquired their Freemasonry during their residence in Palestine. Some writers go so far as to say that the degree of Prince of Lebanon, the twenty-second in the Ancient and Accepted Scottish Rite, refers to the ancestors of these mystical mountaineers in Syria.

Duad. The number two in the Pythagorean system of numbers. See *Two.*

Dualism. In the old mythologies, there was a doctrine which supposed the world to have been always governed by two antagonistic principles, distinguished as the good and the evil principle. This doctrine pervaded all the Oriental religions.

Thus in the system of Zoroaster we have Ahriman and Ormuzd, and in the Hebrew cosmogony we fi'nd the Creator and the Serpent. There has been a remarkable development of this system in the three degrees of Symbolic Masonry, which everywhere exhibit in their organization, their symbolism, and their design, the pervading influences of this principle of dualism. Thus, in the first degree, there is Darkness overcome by Light; in the second, Ignorance dispersed by Knowledge, and in the third, Death conquered by Eternal Life.

Dub. In the ancient ceremonies of chivalry, a knight was made by giving him three strokes on the neck with the flat end cf the sword, and he was then said to be "dubbed a knight." Dubbing is from the Saxon, *dubban,* to strike with a blow. Sir Thomas Smith *(Eng. Commonwealth),* who wrote in the sixteenth century, says: "And when any man is made a knight, he, kneeling down, is strooken of the prince, with his sword naked, upon the back or shoulder, the prince saying, *Sits* or *sois chevalier au nom de Dieu,* and (in times past) they added St. George, and at his arising the prince sayeth, *Avancey.* This is the manner of *dubbing* of knights at this present; a'nd that terme *dubbing* was the old terme in this point, and not *creation."*

Due East and West. A Lodge is said to be situated due East and West for reasons which have varied at different periods in the ritual and lectures. See *Orientation.*

Due Examination. That sort of examination which is correct and prescribed by law. It is one of the three modes of proving a strange brother; the other two being *strict trial* and *lawful information.* See *Vouching.*

182
CHURCH
CHRISTIANIZATION

Christianization of Freemasonry.
The interpretation of the symbols of Freemasonry from a Christian point of view is a theory adopted by some of the most distinguished Masonic writers of England and this country, but one which I think does not belong to the ancient system. Hutchinson, and after him Oliver,—profoundly philosophical as are the Masonic speculations of both,—have, I nrn constrained to believe, fallen into a great error in calling the Master Mason's degree a Christian institution. It is true that it I embraces within its scheme the great I truths of Christianity upon the subject I of the immortality of the soul and the resurrection of the body; but this was to be presumed, because Freemasory ' is truth, and all truth must be iden- i tical. But the origin of each is different; their histories are dissimilar. The principles of Freemasonry preceded the advent of Christianity. Its symbols and its legends are derived from the i Solomonic Temple and from the people j even anterior to that. Its religion | comes from the ancient priesthood; its [faith was that primitive one of Noah | and his immediate descendants. If Masonry were simply a Christian institution, the Jew and the Moslem, the Brahman and the Buddhist, could not conscientiously partake of its illumination. But its universality is its boast. In its language citizens of every nation mav converse; at its altar men of all religions may kneel; to its creed disciples of every faith may subscribe.

Yet it cannot be denied that since the advent of Christianity a Christian element has been almost imperceptibly infused into the Masonic system, at least among Christian Masons. This has been a necessity; for it is the tendency of every predominant religion to pervade with its influence all that surrounds it or is about it, whether religious, political, or social. This arises from a need of the human heart. To the man deeply imbued with the spirit of his religion, there is an almost unconscious desire to accommodate and adapt all the business and the amusements of life,—the labors and the employments of his every-day existence,— to the in-dwelling faith of his soul.

The Christian Mason, therefore, while acknowledging and appreciating the great doctrines taught in Masonry, and also while

> grateful that these doctrines were preserved in the bosom of his ancient Order at a time when they were unknown to the multitudes of the surrounding nations, is still anxious to give to them a Christian character; to invest them, in some measure, with the peculiarities of his own creed, and to bring the interpretation of their symbolism more nearly home to his own religious sentiments.
>
> The feeling is an instinctive one, belonging to the noblest aspirations of our human nature; and hence we find Christian Masonic writers indulging in it to an almost unwarrantable excess, and, by the extent of their sectarian interpretations, materially affecting the cosmopolitan character of the Institution.
>
> This tendency to Christianization has, in some instances, been so universal, and has prevailed for so long *a* period, that certain symbols and myths have been in this way, so deeply and thoroughly imbued with the Christian element as to leave those who have not penetrated into the cause of this peculiarity, in doubt whether they should attribute to the symbol an ancient or a modern and Christian origin.

Wicca and Masonry

Wiccans draw comparisons of masonry with their own occult practices. On a homepage for Wicca, they reveal:

- They both have a foundational system of three degrees, with some forms of Wicca offering higher degrees after achieving the third degree.
- Both are secret societies because they keep their membership rolls secret and secrets are kept from the general public by both religions.
- Both usually meet in secret with the exceptions for the purpose of rare openly public events.
- Both have ceremonial forms of purging and purifications of the ritual area before commencing any ritual work.
- They both have the candidates remove all secular clothing, remove all metal (jewelry, etc.) and are hoodwinked (blindfolded) with ropes ceremonially tied around them.
- Both groups have the candidate stand in the Northeast corner of the temple in the first degree.

- Both groups challenge the candidate by piercing their naked chest with a sharp implement (witches utilize the sword while Masons use the point of a compass.)
- They both challenge the candidate by asking for secret passwords.
- Both have the candidate lead in a circular walk around the temple while hoodwinked.
- Both have the candidate (while hoodwinked) endure being picked up, carried around, spun around, pushed or struck from one person to another that is supposed to create an "altered state of consciousness in the candidate."
- Both have the ceremonial un-hoodwinking of the candidate after he has taken the oath, before lighted candles that are supposed to bring illumination.
- Both explain to the new initiate the "working tools" pertaining to that degree and each tool's use is taught to the initiate.
- Both groups, in the higher degrees, bring the candidate through a "from-death-to-rebirth" ritual in which he acts the part of the hero of the craft.

A study of the temple arrangement of both groups easily brings to mind the Osage secret society of Little Old Men. The seven degrees and accompanying rituals have remarkable similarities to both Masonry and Wicca. Solomon was right. There is nothing new under the sun.

To be quite fair, I must finish Dr. Clark's story. After he viewed the videotape and was very upset, he never spoke of Masonry again. In the years my mother had been he and his wife's nurse, Dr. Clark had always proudly noted his 33rd degree honorary status to anyone who would listen. Following his death in March of 2001, the funeral home operator, also a Mason, had dressed Dr. Clark's remains in the typical Masonic lambskin apron. Dr. Clark's daughter protested. "Take that thing off him. Daddy didn't want that on him and he didn't want the Masons to have anything to do with his funeral." He took the apron off, and the Masons didn't have anything to do with his funeral.

Eglinton Colony

The Eglinton Colony of Taney County was founded through a national organization called the Knights of Labor of North America. In 1880, a group from the colony in New York decided to head to Texas to pursue development of a socialist colony. On the way, they made a train stop in Springfield, Missouri and learned of good opportunities for development in Taney County. Four families decided to cast their lot in Taney County while the remaining eight families agreed to travel on to Texas. Somewhere along the journey they had fallen into the influence of Henry E. Sharpe who had purchased 522 acres of land near present day Taneyville. This is where they chose to settle. Later, most of the families who had continued on to Texas returned to Taney County and rejoined their colony family. By mid 1888, the colony had failed and while some members moved from the area, others like John T. and Mary Dickenson integrated into Taney County society and became successful store owners. The Dickenson's were brutally assaulted in April 1885 by Frank and Tubal Taylor. Although they survived, their attackers were dragged from the Taney County jail and hung in an explosive act of vigilante justice. Just over a year later in September 1886, John T. Dickenson was made a member of the Forsyth Masonic Lodge.

Further evidence of the Masonic connection with Eglinton is revealed in the *Encyclopedia of Freemasonry*:

> Eglinton Manuscript--an Old Record supposed to be of the date of 1599. It is so named from its having been discovered some years ago in the charter chest at Eglinton Castle. It is a Scottish manuscript, and is valuable for its details of early Masonry in Scotland. In it, Edinburgh is termed "the first and principal lodge," and Kilwinning is called "the heid and second Ludge of Scotland in all tyme cuming." An exact copy of it was taken by Brother D. Murray Lyon, and first published by Brother W.J. Hughan in his Unpublished Records of the Craft.

Modern Woodmen

A couple of years after I researched the section on Freemasonry, a man asked me what I knew about Modern Woodmen. I was stumped having never heard of them. However, shortly I found in the Thursday, April 13, 1905 edition of the *Taney County Republican* this notice:

> M.W.A.—Forsyth Camp No. 8650 meets on Tuesday upon or first following the full moon each month. J.V. Baldwin, Head Counsel. C.H. Groom, Clerk.

I made an inquiry to the Modern Woodmen headquarters and received a letter from them in January of 2000 indicating that a camp at Forsyth, No. 8650 was chartered September 12, 1900, and dissolved on October 16, 1930. Gail Ann Levis, historian for the organization, admitted to me via a telephone interview they "*used to have secret adoption rituals.*" However, she insisted these rituals were ended in 1965, and Modern Woodmen functions as a fraternal order for the purpose of offering life insurance benefits to members.

Cults

The rugged hills have often been home to small bands of the deceived who follow strange beliefs and often suffer the consequences. Ozarks native, Douglas Mahnkey wrote in his book, *Bright Glowed My Hills:*

> Down my way they still talk about how, along about 1910, a group of mountaineers in the Bull Creek Country set up a pagan organization for the worship of God. They practiced nudism. A band of them—men, women and children—completely unclad, attempted to parade through Forsyth. I know this is true for I have seen a picture that a photographer took of the group, about twenty in all, as they emerged from the cane brakes of Swan Creek and started walking into the public square. The sheriff and his deputies, along with several outraged citizens, broke up the parade and put the leaders in jail. Judge John T. Moore was on the bench, as I recall the story, when the first defendant was brought to trial. The man refused to accept a defense lawyer the court had offered to appoint but shouted that 'the Lord would look after me—I'm in the Lord's hands!' Judge Moore listened to him for a little while then sentenced him to a year in jail.

CHAPTER TEN

MORMONISM

"Before I learned the hidden history of Mormonism, there were things that bothered me such as, for example, the guilt-tripping sermons aimed squarely at the ones who attended faithfully." Former Mormon

Out of respect for my son's friendship during his teen years with a boy who was being raised Mormon, and the hope that I could win the young man to Jesus Christ alone, I declined to write about this subject in the first edition of my book. I believe, however, there is unfinished business here and so I am impressed to write about the subject of Mormons and their connection both historically and currently to our region. It is my sincere hope that we can still reach these precious people with the truth.

In 1998 I dreamed I was in an old gas station when I needed to use the restroom. After I came out of the station, there were four women lining the sidewalk where I was intending to walk. Although it was daytime, they were holding unlit candles. Each wore a dark cape with the hood pulled up over their heads. As I passed by, they averted their eyes, but I caught glimpses of their name tags. Even in my dream I remember trying to memorize their names, but by the time I awoke I could not remember them. It was a strange dream, so I mentioned it to my husband.

During that period of time, our church was experiencing a great move of God. Souls were mightily being touched and changed. We had revival services almost every night. That night we attended services, as was our custom. During our worship time, I felt a group of people come in and sit in one of the pews somewhere behind me. I turned to glance at them and was stunned to see four women seated, each wearing a custom name tag that identified them as members of the Church of Jesus Christ of Latter Day Saints. The title "sister" preceded their individual names.

When it was time for the preaching to begin, they all filed out and headed for the ladies restroom. I followed them. When I got inside the restroom, they were clumped together by the sinks. They were startled when they saw me, but I just stuck my hand out to shake their hands and greet them. They declined my extended hand, turned quickly and walked out of the restroom and on out of the church.

Of course, my attention was drawn to research Mormonism. I soon discovered their rituals were strikingly similar to Freemasonry. In 1994 when I was working in the business community, I had occasion to visit a boutique in one of the area shopping centers. In conversation with the owner she began to tell me why she was in Branson. She explained that some of the Apostles of the Church of Jesus Christ of Latter Day Saints had received revelation that the original Garden of Eden was here in Taney County. Thus, that would be where Christ would make his triumphant return to earth and set up His eternal kingdom. The Mormons were buying large tracts of Taney County property in order to prepare for this event. At the time, I had brushed off her story as "nuts." But now I came back to that. Why was the Lord drawing my attention to Mormons via this dream? Why had these four women visited our church in such a strange manner? What did Mormons have to do with our land and people?

My research began with the Mormons dishonorable expulsion from our state. Governor W. Boggs issued a violent extermination or expulsion order on October 27, 1838. "The Mormons must be treated as enemies," Boggs declared, "and must be exterminated or driven from the State if necessary for the public peace; their outrages are beyond all description." Three days later, a unit of the state militia killed 17 men and boys, all members of the Church of Jesus Christ of Latter Day Saints, in the Haun's Mill Massacre. My husband's family has a personal historical connection to this terrible time in our state's history. Steve's great-great grandfather, Brigadier General James H. Graham, of Lexington, Missouri, commanded a state militia brigade charged with the expulsion of the Mormons.

During my research, I also discovered that in 1976 Governor Kit Bond had formally rescinded the order expressing "deep regret for the injustice and undue suffering which was caused by Governor Bogg's order." The rescission noted that the 1838 order "clearly contravened the rights to life, liberty, property and religious freedom as guaranteed by the Constitution of the United States as well as the Constitution of the State of Missouri."

My research also showed we had a regional connection to the Mormons. On May 13, 1857, in Alma, Arkansas, Parley P. Pratt, one of the 12 Mormon apostles, was killed by Hector McLean. Pratt had usurped the marriage of McLean and his wife Eleanor, taking her as his 12th plural wife. This incident led to an outraged McLean stabbing then shooting Pratt who died a few hours later from loss of blood. Word arrived in Utah of the murder making Pratt yet another martyr to the Mormons who had been chased out of both Missouri and Illinois.

Two months earlier, in March of 1857, a wagon train of Southern Missouri and Northern Arkansas families met at Caravan Springs on Highway 7 near Harrison to begin their journey west to California. They never arrived. In Utah at an area now known as Mountain Meadows, 120 of the 137 hopeful immigrants were slaughtered in a bloody massacre led by Mormons and assisted by Paiute Indians. Only 17 children deemed too young to tell were spared. They were divided among Mormon households. Over a year later, they were finally rescued and returned to relatives.

On August 25, 1940, *The American Weekly* published Mrs. Sallie Baker Mitchell's eye witness account:

> I'm the only person still living who was in that massacre, where the Mormons and the Indians attacked a party of 137 settlers on the way to California, murdering everybody except 17 children, who were spared because they were all under eight years of age. I was one of those children and when the killing started I was sitting on my daddy's lap in one of the wagons. The same bullet that snuffed out his life took a nick out of my left ear, leaving a scar you can see to this day.
>
> Last November, I passed my 85th birthday and at the time of the massacre I wasn't quite three years old. But even when you're that young, you don't forget the horror of having your father gasp for breath and grow limp, while you have your arms around his neck, screaming with terror. You don't forget the blood-curdling

war-whoops and the banging of guns all around you. You don't forget the screaming of the other children and the agonized shrieks of women being hacked to death with tomahawks. And you wouldn't forget it, either, if you saw your own mother topple over in the wagon beside you, with a big red splotch getting bigger and bigger on the front of her calico dress.

When the massacre started, Mother had my baby brother, Billy, in her lap and my two sisters, Betty and Mary Levina, were sitting in the back of the wagon. Billy wasn't quite two, Betty was about five and Vina was eight.

We never knew what became of Vina. Betty saw some Mormons leading her over the hill, while the killing was still going on. Betty, Billy and I were taken to a Mormon home and kept there till the soldiers rescued us, along with the other children, about a year later, and carried us back to our folks in Arkansas. Captain James Lynch was in charge of the soldiers who found us...I never will forget the day we finally got back to Arkansas. You would have thought we were heroes. They had a buggy parade for us through Harrison.

When we got around to our house, Grandma Baker, the one who refused to go to California, was standing on the porch. She was a stout woman and mighty dignified, too. When we came along the road leading up to the house she was pacing back and forth but when she caught sight of us she ran down the path and grabbed hold of us, one after the other and gave us a powerful hug.

> Leah, our old Negro mammy, caught me up in her arms and wouldn't let me go. She carried me around all the rest of the day, even cooking supper with me in her arms. I remember she baked each of us children a special little apple turn-over pie. We had creamed potatoes for supper that night, too, and they sure tasted good. I've been especially fond of creamed potatoes ever since.
>
> I remember I called all of the women I saw "mother." I guess I was still hoping to find my own mother, and every time I called a woman "mother," she would break out crying.

William Tackett, another one of the children spared, was returned to relatives in Arkansas. After he married, he moved to Taney County where he died near Protem in the summer of 1893. His grave in the lonely cemetery near the White River is marked by a tombstone bearing the inscription: "One of the survivors of the Mountain Meadow Massacre."

Missouri relatives of those massacred connected the terrible event to retaliation for the Mormon expulsion in 1838. Arkansas relatives connected the event to retaliation for McLean's killing of Pratt in Alma, Arkansas.

What a sad chapter in our history! In modern times, Mormon Church officials have acknowledged this tragedy and offered an apology which is noted and appreciated. I am not including this section to inflame hearts against any group of people. We all have much for which we should apologize and repent. I believe I am prompted to include it so that we might know that the spirits behind this deceptive religion have historical roots here which continue to be fed by those roots.

I have personally known Mormons whom I have found to be gentle and kind. However, I grieve for the deception they are under. Jesus Christ needs no other gospel than the one He brought when He staked His own life to the cross. That a deceived man such as Joseph Smith should author "another" gospel which continues to undergo revisions to suit the members over time, is proof of the changeable nature of man. It is no proof at all of the nature of Our Unchanging God. The Holy Scriptures of the Old Testament and New Testament are quite enough. No man-made religious practices can supersede the power of the Truth. The key difference between true Christianity and the deceptions of the Mormon Church can be found in one phrase, "In Christ Alone."

Note the deception in this 1856 sermon by Brigham Young:

> There are sins that men commit for which they cannot receive forgiveness in this world, or in that which is to come, and if they had their eyes open to see their true condition, they would be perfectly willing to have their blood spilt upon the ground, that the smoke thereof might ascend to heaven as an offering for their sins; and the smoking incense would atone for their sins, whereas, if such is not the case, they will stick to them and remain upon them in the spirit world. I know when you hear my brethren telling about cutting people off from the earth that you consider it is strong doctrine; but it is to save them, not to destroy them.... And further more, I know that there are transgressors, who, if they knew themselves, and the only condition upon which they can obtain forgiveness, would beg of

> their brethren to shed their blood, that the smoke thereof might ascend to God as an offering to appease the wrath that is kindled against them, and that the law might have its course. I will say further; I have had men come to me and offer their lives to atone for their sins. It is true that the blood of the Son of God was shed for sins through the fall and those committed by men, yet men can commit sins which it can never remit.... There are sins that can be atoned for by an offering upon an altar, as in ancient days; and there are sins that the blood of a lamb, or a calf, or of turtle dove, cannot remit, but they must be atoned for by the blood of the man.

In an online article, *What Shocked You the Most?* a former Mormon wrote:

> Before I learned the hidden history of Mormonism, there were things that bothered me such as, for example, the guilt-tripping sermons aimed squarely at the ones who attended faithfully. In fact, I was in one of my most TBM [Mormon] phases when I began to search the Internet. I'd heard at least two different NPR programs; one on polygamy, and one on the Mountain Meadows Massacre and blood atonement. I was unprepared for the volume of knowledge that hit me like a flash flood; it swept my foundation completely away.
>
> I think what shocked me the most was the extent of Joseph Smith's polygamy - marrying teenagers, other men's wives, and doing it under the pretext of a divine threat, etc. I was blown

away by the church's lack of honesty in portraying its history. As I learned the truth about the Book of Abraham, the facts about Native American DNA, Freemasonry and the endowment, different versions of the first vision, Smith's background with "seer stones" and money-digging, it all fell apart. I was appalled by the barbarity of Brigham Young - his teachings on blood atonement, his support of violence, as in the Bishop Snow incident, his racism, and his condescension toward women. I lost all confidence in Gordon Hinckley when I heard him say in regard to a key Mormon doctrine, "I don't know that we teach it. I don't know that we emphasize it." When I finally came out to my bishop in 2003, he said I should study and pray more and my former stake president stated "you can have doubts but if you ever teach anyone about them, you know what I'll have to do." I was incensed. I wrote my resignation letter that very night and I sent it in eight months later.

It's been just over four years since discovering the truth. DW [dear wife] still tells me that she misses me at church and people ask about me. Funny, I still live in the same house and I have the same phone number. No one is really that curious to call me or stop by for a visit. I suppose I am anathema to most TBMs and that's fine with me.

I believe there is some unfinished business in the areas of repentance, forgiveness, and reconciliation. I believe these dear people need the opportunity to escape the darkness and come into the light of Jesus Christ—the Jesus Christ we serve who needs no "other" gospel than the one upon which He staked His life and whose atonement was enough for us all forever.

CHAPTER ELEVEN

THE BALDKNOBBERS

"Fer as I'm consarned they're a beam-eyed society for the eradication of motes."
Parson Dennison, 1885

To fully understand the great shame of the Bald Knobber era, one must view the conditions particular to Taney County just before this infamous vigilante group was formed. In his book co-written with Mary Hartman, *Bald Knobbers, Vigilantes on the Ozarks Frontier,* Elmo Ingenthron wrote, "From it's inception in 1837 to the outbreak of the Civil War, the county recorded three murders. Between 1865 and1885 there were said to have been between 30-40 murders."

Constable A.G. Layton posted a public notice in the March 1, 1883 edition of the *Taney Enterprise:*

> From this date, whenever any person comes to Forsyth and gets drunk or raises a disturbance, I will incarcerate him, her or them in the county jail without ceremony.

The irony of this posting was that six months later on September 22, 1883, A.G. Layton rode to Forsyth after helping dig a diversion ditch on Jim and Barton (Yell) Everett's mill on Bull Creek. There, he got into a drunken brawl with another man in Jim Everett's saloon. Jim broke up the brawl but Layton pulled his revolver and shot Jim in the chest. Jim's brother Barton, (nicknamed Yell), his Uncle Emmett, and Charles H. Groom were eyewitnesses to the murder.

Early 1884. Alexander C. Kissee found three of his cattle dead of starvation. Their tongues had been chopped out. Kissee suspected Frank and Tubal Taylor with whom he had trouble before. A sheriff's warrant was issued for Tubal but he escaped.

October 7, 1884. Newton W. Herrell killed his mother's lover, Amus Ring. Herrell's mother, the only witness, signed a murder complaint.

October 18, 1884. Layton was acquitted for the murder of Jim Everett. Rumors said T. C. Spellings, prosecutor, (and publisher of the newspaper), accepted a bribe to "go easy on Al."

Furious that criminals were not being properly brought to trial and questioning the financial management of county resources, thirteen men formed the "Citizens Committee for Law and Order," a secret oath bound society. These men included:

- "Captain" Nat Kinney, who initiated the "committee"
- James Delong, Nat's step-son
- Alonzo Prather, Taney County State Representative
- Yell (Barton) Everett, brother to murder victim
- James B. Rice
- T. W. Phillips
- James R. Van Zandt, former State Representative (1882-1884) and Methodist Minister
- Pat Fickle
- Galba Branson, brother to Reuben Branson and sheriff from 1888-1889
- J.J. Brown, attorney
- Charles H. Groom, attorney, also held various county offices, including Taney County Treasurer, 1884-1886

- James K. Polk McHaffie, sheriff from 1884-1888
- B. B. Price, attorney

Oddly, membership into the "secret oath bound society" quickly exploded. On April 5, 1885, Kinney extended membership to 87 more men. They established a night time meeting place on a bald knob near the Oak Grove School. Old timers claimed that is how the group got their name, the Bald Knobbers.

Three days later, frequent troublemakers Frank and Tubal Taylor shot and left for dead John and Mary Dickenson who were storekeepers of the Eglinton Colony, Taney City (now Taneyville). Dickenson and his wife both survived. However, one hundred men were primed for revenge. On April 15, 1885, vigilante violence exploded. The Bald Knobbers surrounded the county jail under cover of darkness, killed the young deputy on duty, dragged the Taylors out of jail and hanged them from an oak tree. An old settler, John Ingenthron, found their bodies the next morning. I wonder if he considered the scripture in Deuteronomy 21:23 that warns against the desecration of the land, "You must not leave his body on the tree overnight. Be sure to bury him that same day, because anyone who is hung on a tree is under God's curse. You must not desecrate the land the LORD your God is giving you as an inheritance."

Madison Day, a former Bald Knobber and later one who served as sheriff after Sheriff Galba Branson was killed, offered this eye witness report. "The tree was a mile and a half down Walnut Shade Road. The horses crossed Swan Creek and turned left. The caravan swarmed up the hill near Riverview School. The grisly expedition wended northwesterly toward Walnut Shade, traveling nearly two miles before arriving at a tree atop a ridge near Cedar Point" (Ingenthron).

Immediately following the vigilante hanging, Alonzo Prather, Charles Groom and J.J. Brown withdrew from the "Citizen's Committee."

Note the quick growth and progressively bolder violence:

1885-Summer. Popular leader Nat Kinney helped Douglas and Christian Counties organize their own "law and order league."

1885-December 19. County courthouse destroyed by arsonist fire. Most suspected Bald Knobbers. An important land record volume was rescued by Charles Groom, a former Bald Knobber.

1886-February. Kinney killed unarmed, 19-year-old Andrew Coggburn outside of Oak Grove Church after Kinney preached the Sunday sermon.

On March 1, 1886, the day after Nat Kinney shot Andrew Coggburn, former county judge John J. Reynolds said the citizens realized it was time to take action. Jurd Haworth, the pastor of the Pleasant Hill Christian Church and Master of the Forsyth Masonic Lodge since 1877 made an impassioned plea to local citizens urging the cessation of violence. The men agreed to form a home guard. They petitioned the Governor to declare Taney County under martial law and arm the local home guards, bring in the state militia and drive out the Bald Knobbers. A committee consisting of Judge Reynolds, Jurd Haworth and Dr. Burdette was appointed to travel to Jefferson City and submit the petition. Pastor Haworth and Dr. Burdette later backed out so brave Judge Reynolds traveled alone to see the Governor.

1886-March. Governor ordered the Bald Knobbers to disband

1886- April 10. 500 Bald Knobbers met at Forsyth to publicly disband. However floggings, shootings and arson against victims continued.

1886-May. Kinney's bodyguard, Wash Middleton, killed Sam Snapp, the unarmed father of five young children, on steps of the general store in Kirbyville. Sam Snapp was Andrew Coggburn's friend and Anti-Bald Knobber sympathizer.

1886-November. Bald Knobbers held onto most county seats in a bitter election. Charles Groom lost his seat as Taney County Treasurer.

1887-March. Chadwick, Missouri Bald Knobbers killed two men and injured their wives and children in what is known as Edens-Green murders. C.O. Simmons, Chadwick (Christian County) pastor, was among those charged with the bloody attack on the sleeping families.

1887-June. Robert Meadows was murdered.

1887-July. W.O. Evans was shot and killed.

1887-July. Mack Dimmock was murdered.

1888-July 4. Jim Holt, a Lead Hill detective hired by Sam Snapp's brothers hunted down and killed Wash Middleton.

1888-August. Billy, Emanuel and Jim Miles (ages 20, 18, and 16 respectively) killed "Captain" Nat Kinney, in Forsyth. Billy was the actual shooter.

1888-November. America Pruitt supposedly murdered her two young daughters and supposedly slashed her throat ending her own life. One account says she "was distraught over violence of the Bald Knobbers."

1889-May. Christian County hung three Bald Knobbers for Edens-Green murders.

1889-July 4. At a picnic in Kirbyville, Billy, Jim and Emanuel Miles escaped after killing Bald Knobber sheriff, Galba Branson and hired gun, Ed Funk who had purposed to avenge Nat Kinney's death.

1889-July. James Dennis was murdered.

1889-November. Walter Jones was murdered.

1891-July. Sam Lee was murdered.

1892-March. John Wesley Bright shot and killed his wife and left her body for the hogs to eat. Two days later, he was dragged out of the Forsyth jail and hung. The lynch mob killed young Deputy Williams in the vigilante attack.

No chapter like this in any region's history could have been penned without the charismatic leadership of someone like "Captain" Nat Kinney. Kinney, who was no captain at all, had migrated to Taney County from Springfield, MO. Perhaps his sudden change of address had something to do with the $1,500 of taxpayer's money he pocketed from an unpopular civil suit against the City of Springfield because Kinney had supposedly fallen from the sidewalk and injured his leg. The City of Springfield asserted that his drunken state contributed to his accident, not the condition of the city's sidewalk. Nevertheless, this larger-than-life figure entered Taney County with a pocket full of cash and within a few short years became its most enduring legendary figure.

Eye witnesses remembered Nat Kinney as tall, nearly six-and-a-half feet in his socks, thick and muscular, fierce in countenance, with a red head and a burly red beard, reminiscent of Thor, son of Viking god Odin. Nat Kinney was a religious man who often bragged that he had started the county's first Sunday school (although one had actually been ongoing two years earlier). He was a preacher who exhorted from Biblical texts with his six-shooter lying on the pulpit beside him. He was a fine orator who loved an audience and loved the power he enjoyed. However, he was ruthless and cruel.

"According to Harvey Castleman (early historian), citizens were not lacking who alleged that Kinney and his outlaws had killed more than thirty men and at least four women. And not one of Kinney's riders had been punished for a single murder" (Ingenthron).

In the *Springfield Republican* the editor wrote, "Whatever may have been Kinney's influence in the lawless order everybody believes that but for his leadership the Bald Knob organization would never have existed. He was responsible, it is believed, for all the lawlessness of Southwest Missouri. In his death, the Southwest has been cleared of the root of evil which has been its curse. Although deploring crime and violence, the majority of our people say Amen!"

BALD KNOBBER OATH UNTO DEATH

In the first mass meeting of the "Law and Order League" on April 5, 1885, between one hundred and two hundred men gathered around as Nat Kinney read a long list of crimes and immoral acts in his view the courts had left unpunished. He recounted the disregard of social proprieties such as men living with women to whom they had never been married.

After agitating the crowd to his satisfaction, Kinney asked attorney J.J. Brown to read aloud the oath of admission. The crowd was instructed to form circles consisting of 13 men each and clasp each other's hands while they swore in unison:

> Do you in the presence of God and these witnesses, solemnly swear that you will never reveal any of the secrets of this order nor communicate any part of it to any person or persons in the known world, unless you are satisfied by a strict test or in some legal way that they are rightfully entitled to receive them; that you will conform and abide by the rules and

> regulations of this order and obey all orders of your superior officers or any brother officer under whose jurisdiction you may be at the time attached; nor will you propose for membership or sanction the admission of anyone whom you have reason to believe is not worthy of being a member; nor will you oppose the admission of anyone solely on a personal matter? You shall report all theft that is made known to you and not leave unreported any theft on account of his being blood relations of yours; nor will you willfully report anyone through personal enmity. You shall recognize and answer all signs made by lawful brothers and render them such assistance as they may be in need of, so far as you are able or the interest of your family will permit; nor will you willfully wrong or defraud a brother or permit it if in your power to prevent it. Should you willfully and knowingly violate this oath in any way, you subject yourself to the jurisdiction of twelve members of this order, even if their decision should be to hang you by the neck until you are dead, dead, dead. So help me God.

Kinney drilled the participants in secret grips and passwords. Neither Kinney nor Brown had ever belonged to the Masonic Order, although they allegedly designed the recognition challenges based on the Mason's strange rituals (Hartman and Ingenthron).

A half dozen violent and frightful years passed before the Bald Knobber violence was quelled. After the Edens-Green murders in Christian County and the subsequent hangings by the murderous perpetrators, the national spotlight was shined on the shameful actions of the vigilantes. This brought into the light the evil deeds which had been done in the darkness.

Years later, Charles H. Groom's heroic actions during the courthouse fire would prove to be the critical link to uncovering the real motive behind these dreadful years. Groom had awakened to the cries of "Fire!" Clad only in his nightshirt and boots, he raced to the Taney County courthouse and around to his office window. He quickly broke the glass and snatched a valuable land record volume off his desk, the only official court record to survive the inferno. This document which was held quietly for years stands today as an indictment against many known Bald Knobbers and reveals the truth behind their twisted idea of "justice."

There are many accounts of Bald Knobbers, "riding against" a family for some real or imagined slight or crime. A bundle of switches, tossed upon the victim's porch was a signal to them, "Clear out or face the wrath of the Citizens Committee!" Neighbors would lie trembling in bed while they heard the midnight rattle of their neighbor's wagon wheels upon the creek beds or rough trails during their terrified night flight.

Soon afterward, a Bald Knobber's name would appear in the land record as the new homesteader, claiming that the former homesteader had "abandoned his claim before proving his rights."

The I. J. Haworth Story

J. Haworth's story took place near Forsyth, Missouri, and was recorded years later for the centennial issue of the Taney County newspaper, but for some unknown reason never published.

As I have told you, I have been here since 1873. It was necessary for everyone to be on one side or the other and I took the side of the Anti Bald Knobbers. I was outspoken and didn't care who I told this to, although I was criticized by many. I managed to rent a farm ten miles below Forsyth, known as the Dick Moore Farm. I had a long lease on it, even though some of the Bald Knobbers wanted the farm and I rented one of them 15 acres in the lower end of the field, and he planted corn. There was a lot of the land not cleared at the lower end of the field, (bout 50 acres), the end that I had rented. Hogs broke in and ruined a lot of his corn. He hired a man to go down and kill some of the hogs, which he did. The Bald Knobbers laid this on me since I lived on the place. I had the place rented for the next year although several Bald Knobbers wanted it. They could not get it if I wanted to stay, so they decided to scare me out of living on the place. The next year I still kept possession of the place but I didn't live on it. I stayed at my uncles. About 20 Bald Knobbers came to my home one evening, on horseback. They kept pretty well hidden by the woods and other buildings on the place. One of the horsemen rode up to the gate and called me out. He said his name was McGill and asked, "Are you going to tend that farm down there again?" I said, "Yes Sir, I am." He replied, "We have come to notify you that you can't do it." I told him, "I'll tend that place if every ear of corn cost me a dollar." He said, "If you want to do that we will crack your neck." Guns from other Bald Knobbers who were hidden in the shadows of the buildings started roaring, shooting into the roof of the house. They turned around and rode off and went about a mile south of where I lived to Ed Boyd's, took him out and whipped the britches off him.

Haworth wasn't the only person to assess the Bald Knobber years as a thinly guised land grab. One day I was busy in my office when another divine appointment occurred. The phone rang, and the caller explained that she had a small nursing facility in Nixa. One of her patients, Ila Miles DeClue, claimed to be a relative of the Miles brothers who had killed Captain Nat Kinney of the Bald Knobbers. The caller felt I might be interested in interviewing her because her aging patient had written the family's story of this time period. I was and I did. One day I had the good fortune to meet Ila Miles DeClue who was the daughter of Emanuel Miles, the second son of William Miles.

"Captain Kinney sent word to my grand daddy that he wanted him and his three oldest sons to join." William Miles's reply was a vehement refusal. "We ain't angels but we ain't devils neither," he told the messenger. "We will never join you!" Ila said the trouble began in earnest. "They killed Granddad's stock at night and made trouble for the three boys everywhere they went."

Ingenthron and Hartman wrote, "At first few ignored the Bald Knobber's veiled threats. Then resistance grew, and the night riders began to waylay and capture those who ignored the bundle of switches. Occasional shooting matches broke out, with casualties on both sides, especially when several victims banded together for self-defense. Ultimately, however, the Bald Knobbers captured their man and took him into the woods. They stripped him, tied him to a tree, and applied a black snake whip or hickory gad (a spear or wand). The stubborn victims suffered as many as two hundred lashes. Some were left unconscious and covered with blood.

"The anti-Bald Knobbers didn't believe in killing innocent men, hurting their wives, taking their hogs and pigs out and selling them and keeping the money. That's the Bald Knobbers for you! Dad said they did it!" vowed Ila.

Ila's clan was one of the largest and oldest family groups in the county. They had "married up" to several other large family clans who were vehemently Anti-Bald Knobber. Perhaps this emboldened William Miles and his sons.

"The word came to the Miles' brothers again—join!" Ila said, "Granddad told Billy, 'keep the gun a shining and if you ever have to shoot, don't let the Captain get his gun first.'" Kinney persisted and demanded that Miles's sons Billy, age 20, Emanuel, age 18, and Jim, age 16, come and see him. "Billy got to the store where Captain Kinney was and he said, "I'm Billy Miles. You sent for me?" Captain said, "I sure did. Did you come to join?" Billy said, "I'll die first!" Captain reached for his guns and Billy shot him several times. They heard him hollering all over Forsyth."

Billy gave himself up to Sheriff McHaffie, one of the original thirteen Bald Knobbers who had become disenchanted with the organization shortly after the vigilante hanging of the Taylor brothers. According to Ila, "Billy said, 'I just killed Captain Kinney in self-defense.'" Jim was outside "around the back" but Ila doesn't know whether her father, Emmanuel, had obeyed the Captain's summons and went to town that day. He would never say.

Billy was tried in Springfield on a change of venue and acquitted by the jury. Ironically, his attorney was J.J. Brown, one of the thirteen original Bald Knobbers who had also quit the organization after the Taylor hangings. The prosecuting attorney was James DeLong, who was another original Bald Knobber and also Kinney's stepson.

The Captain was dead, and Billy was a free man. Still the community was rife with tension. Baldknobbers and Anti-Baldknobbers were rattling sabers, speaking of revenge and fearing retaliation. On July 4, 1889, nearly one year after the shooting, the annual Kirbyville picnic attracted many Taney Countians.

"Just before sundown, Rufus Barker, who was a friend (and cousin) of the Miles' boys, heard the Bald Knobbers had a stranger there to kill Billy. Taney County people kept coming up to Billy, warning, 'Stranger in town! Stranger in town!' So they talked it over and decided to leave the picnic before dark, as Billy didn't want to be ambushed," said Ila. Billy, Emanuel, Jim and Elisha, along with Rufus Barker, got their horses and left the picnic grounds.

They stopped at the spring for a drink (the whiskey seemed to be kept there), and while Billy dipped cold water out for some women and children, a man called, "Are you Billy Miles?" Billy responded, "It sure is." The stranger went for his gun, but Billy and Jim shot first. As the stranger fell, his gun discharged, and the bullet hit 16-year-old Jim in the leg.

Meanwhile, Sheriff Galba E. Branson, a known Bald Knobber and one of the original thirteen members, pulled his gun and aimed at Billy. "Dad said never was heard such a mournful sound as he heard from Branson when he shot him. He jumped into the air and fell dead. Dad caught one of Branson's shots in his coattail," said Ila.

It was later told by Branson's widow that the stranger, Ed Funk, hailed from Eureka Springs, Arkansas, and was introduced to her as a U.S. Marshall. Funk in reality was a gunman hired by Kinney's widow to kill Billy Miles. "Branson's widow later told how she tried to keep her husband and Funk from going to the picnic," said Ila. The widow reported that her husband told her to bury them on "that knoll over yonder if the Miles' boys gets us first." Ila took much satisfaction in remembering that two lonesome graves still lie atop that knoll with Branson's and Funk's names on them.

The Miles', along with Rufus Barker, escaped on horseback, helping the wounded Jim between them. Elisha, only a young teenager, was sent home. Rufus was sent to fetch the doctor while the Miles' boys hid at the home of a friend. Rufus returned, reporting that the doctor was too afraid to come. "Dad said, 'I'll go after him and he'll come.' The terrified doctor did come, but was too afraid to treat Jim so the women of the house did their best," said Ila.

Angry Bald Knobbers swept the dense countryside, looking for the boys. Emanuel and Billy stood guard all night. "The next day, Granddad came down with some other men and helped take Jim home," said Ila. William Miles, Sr., sent word that Jim and the other boys were at his home if any of the Bald Knobbers cared to come for them. There were no takers.

After Jim recovered enough to travel, the three brothers walked the sixty miles to Springfield to the home of Rufus Barker's brother. "The boys decided to go down to Virginia to their mother's people," Ila said. However, authorities found Billy and Jim and jailed them in Springfield. Emanuel managed to escape to Virginia by borrowing his girl cousin's clothes. He remained in exile for two years.

Later Jim and Billy were both acquitted. Billy moved to Texas, saying mournfully, "I never shall return to my home in Taney County." Ila said, "He married a Texas girl and that's one Miles I never did see. He never came back." Jim married a Texas girl, too, and had five children. He lived from time to time in Taney County. Ila knew him well and thought he was the most handsome of the brothers, although he had a notorious reputation in Taney County. In 1912, he killed a clerk in the meat market in Branson and spent four years in the state penitentiary. He later moved back to Texas, where he died in 1954 at the age of 83. Emanuel returned to Taney County, where he and his brother Elisha stayed and farmed for most of their lives. Emanuel married Rufus Barker's daughter, Nellie, his second cousin. And in 1902, Ila was born.

Revenge and the greedy lust for land had fed the fire of lawless passions. When the “Captain” died, however, the blaze began to slowly die. Men settled back into the business of developing this wilderness land and providing for their growing families.

When I researched this section of our history, I concerned that I was not being fair. Perhaps the Bald Knobbers had truly and earnestly desired to avenge the murders of innocent lives and set right county financial mismanagement. Perhaps Charles Groom, I. J. Haworth and the Miles family were wrong. Perhaps the whole Baldknobber movement was about balancing the scales of justice. Then one day, I found an obscure *1883* edition of the *Taney Enterprise.* Just one year before the Bald Knobbers were formed, the newspaper had published a story speculating on the potential economic benefits to land holders in Taney County. *The railroad was coming!* The Land of the Osage in the Branson region was about to become more easily accessible and thus, much more valuable.

Lawlessness and greed is a poisonous characteristic which is so often covered with the cloak of self-righteousness. Righteousness outside the constant awareness of the precious, shed blood of Jesus Christ easily becomes self-righteous. Self-righteousness always becomes power and might because, after all, right is on its side. The true motives of the heart: pride, ambition, and greed are often hidden until it is too late. The meek and the weak are so often destroyed when right meets might. Sadly, history repeats itself unless truth is permitted to bring revelation. There in the light and glory of God, both right and might must bow as the laser of God searches the thoughts and intents of the heart.

Parson Dennison had called the Bald Knobbers "a beam-eyed society for the eradication of motes." Jesus said, "And why beholdest thou the mote that is in thy brother's eye, but considerest not the beam that is in thine own eye? Or how wilt thou say to thy brother, Let me pull out the mote out of thine eye; and, behold, a beam is in thine own eye? Thou hypocrite, first cast out the beam out of thine own eye; and then shalt thou see clearly to cast out the mote out of thy brother's eye (Matthew 7:2-5). The Bald Knobbers' initial noble pursuit of justice quickly crashed on the rocks of self-righteousness and hypocrisy. That is the nature of the Pharisee Spirit. This hideous spirit believes that your sin is worse than my sin. However, any true child of God knows that our Father is no respecter of persons. To Him any sin is terrible since it separates us from Him. The Pharisee Spirit also believes that hidden sin can acceptably be ignored while uncovered sin must be dealt with harshly, especially if it is uncovered in someone else by the Pharisee.

Jesus answered this spirit with a truth that is still relevant today. He said we must first examine ourselves and then we can more clearly see how to help someone else. If we don't heed Christ's instruction we will be just as guilty as the Bald Knobbers and just as destructive.

CHAPTER TWELVE

TIME TO CIVILIZE

"Meanwhile the word 'history' drove us to research the history of the city. We looked into the city's layout, its origins, its founders, its social composition and cultural characteristics of the city dwellers." Eduardo Lorenzo

Branson, Missouri, was formally established when a Greene County settler named Reuben Spalding Branson relocated to Taney County. He first settled near the mouth of Bull Creek near present day Rockaway Beach, upon what was once an Indian village site. Within months, Branson moved to the hillside overlooking the White River in what is now known as Downtown Branson. He purchased seven acres from Thomas Jefferson Berry and in 1882 opened a small, general merchandise store. Soon he applied for and received a permit to open an official U. S. Post Office. On the permit application, he named the post office—Branson. As was the custom of the day, that became the name of the fledgling village. Branson's original store building was located near where the old Branson High school building is at 5th and College Streets.

Two years later, Reuben sold his store to William Hawkins and moved to Forsyth, Missouri, where he was elected County Assessor in November, 1884. In 1886 he became County Clerk and Recorder of Deeds during the tumultuous Bald Knobber reign of terror. He was entered a Mason on September 1, 1885. Reuben Spalding lived in

Forsyth most of his life, but returned to Branson shortly before he died in 1935. He was buried with all Masonic rites in the cemetery in Downtown Branson.

While researching the Branson family history, I came upon the heraldic family crest of the Branson family. On the crest was emblazoned the Latin motto, *DUM SPIRO SPERO* (which is also South Carolina's State motto). The meaning of this phrase is:

"Dum Spiro Spero—while I breathe, I hope."

This motto later made an interesting connection in my spirit after I received the vision of the principality that has constricted our people.

Bransons are descendents of the Norse/Viking people who worshipped two principal gods, Thor and Odin. Haven't we been directed to the Vikings before in our research? Odin was the Chief of the gods and ruler of the universe. Odin's sacred bird was the raven/crow. Does this also sound familiar? His principal weapon in addition to his powerful "runes" or magical spells—was the spear. Odin was tall, bearded, and one-eyed, having exchanged his other eye for wisdom.

The Odin cult is apparently characterized by human sacrifice usually accomplished by hanging the victim from an oak tree. As already stated, Reuben Spalding Branson's brother, Galba (often called Galby), was part of the original Bald Knobber's gang who hung the Taylor brothers from an oak tree about two and one half miles northwest of Forsyth, MO. It is also possible, although not historically confirmed, that Reuben participated in the hangings as well.

Thor was the son of Odin and second in importance to him. He was armed with a hammer that returned to his hand after he hurled it at enemies, a belt that doubled

his strength when he wore it, and iron gloves that helped him use the hammer more effectively. Thor was noted for his ability to drink vast amounts of alcohol, depicted as a crude, red-bearded, middle-aged, warrior who relied on strength rather than wits.
(Again, sounding familiar?)

The Branson family is not the only family which offers critical leads into our region's sinful past. The land upon which Branson was first developed may be stained with the blood of murdered men.

Thomas Jefferson Berry was a prominent Taney County citizen in the years following the Civil War. His father, Solomon Berry, was born in North Carolina in 1802 where he also married Lany Linkhorn on December 14, 1829. In 1839, Thomas Jefferson was born in Cape Girardeau, MO. Thomas' mother was Cherokee, and Thomas was a product of the Trail of Tears. At some point during the journey, the Berry family faded out of the detachment they had been traveling with and reappeared in the Missouri Ozarks settling among other mixed bloods.

After the Civil War, Thomas Jefferson Berry filed for a homestead of 160 acres on land that is now part of Downtown Branson. Berry was married three different times. Each wife died, but not before he became the father to nineteen children. He and his sons operated a ferry at the Turkey Creek crossing approximately where the railroad bridge crosses Lake Taneycomo today. He was also a blacksmith.

He became a Mason and later a member of the Bald Knobbers. When Branson arrived in the area, Thomas Jefferson sold seven acres of his property to Reuben, and they became partners in the general store. In 1884, Branson sold his land and interest in the store back to Berry and moved to Forsyth. Berry became partners with

William Marion Hawkins who had recently moved his family from a small cabin on what is now Branson Meadows shopping center. Hawkins became postmaster. His daughter married one of Berry's sons.

By the turn of the century the region was rife with talk about the coming railroad. In 1901 the terrible drought besieged the region. So also did the reports that the St. Louis and Iron Mountain and Southern Railroad would bring its line down Roark Creek and right through Berry's land. Land speculators were already busy. In September 1901, Nathaniel Sterling Maddux, age 70, died of "a protracted illness of dropsy." He owned the land adjacent to and north of Berry's farm. Nathaniel's son, who was also Berry's son-in-law, William Maddux, helped his mother, Charity, organized the sale of the property to Robert E. Lee who later was revealed as the front man for the Branson Town Company.

The Branson Town Company was a Springfield based company of four men who wasted no time in laying out the streets and alleyways for a new town along what they now supposed would be the rail line. In the meantime, Berry and Hawkins were hard at work creating their own development plan. On May 2, 1901, William Hawkins was issued a postal permit for the post office, this time named *Lucia.* They began surveying Berry's land for lots and planning a development they called Lucia.

On February 6, 1902 a brief story, troubling in its modesty, appeared on the front page of the *Taney County Republican.* "Word reaches us after going to press that T.J. Berry committed suicide last night by hanging. Temporary insanity growing out of financial trouble is assigned as the cause."

He was 62 years old. No follow-up story ever appeared in the newspapers. In the *White River Valley Historical Quarterly*, Pearl Hodges, Berry's granddaughter wrote that family members had told her, "T. J. Berry was worried over a debt of $300 which he could not pay during the drought of 1901 and was driven to ill health and eventual suicide."

Privately, however, she surmised to Kathleen Van Buskirk, area author and historian that she believed "her grandfather was murdered." Why would a shrewd man who had survived the Civil War and the Bald Knobber era be distraught over a "debt he could not pay" when he very well knew the railroad was coming through the river valley and thus his property the following year?

His son, Henry Berry, was named administrator of the estate, but in May 1903, he suddenly died at the young age of 34. Again, the newspaper was strangely cryptic. William Maddux, the son-in-law was named by the probate court Judge John T. Dickenson (yes, the one who had been shot by the Taylor brothers, survived and became a Bald Knobber) as administrator, and by August he had sold 35.95 acres to B.B. Price. (Yes, the B.B. Price who was one of the thirteen original Bald Knobbers). Price managed to get the parcel platted and filed by October 2, 1903. The Branson plat was filed on October 26 that same year.

Within months, the members of the Branson Town Company owned both plats and controlled the land that lay along the rail line and most importantly the land that lay within view of the railroad stop. One of the members of the Branson Town Company was a principal in the railroad and another member was a prominent Springfield realtor.

The business district was platted for the upper portion of the land on what are now College and Third Streets. Henry Sullenger purchased the first lot sold for business development. A quickly built cedar, business building soon housed the town's first saloon. The year was 1903. The hamlet of Branson was poised to become a thriving town.

After discovering these interesting facts, I was drawn to the scripture in Habakkuk 2:12 which states, "Woe to him who builds a town with bloodshed; who establishes a city by iniquity." Branson's founding is troubling and suspicious, but I must also consider the silver redemptive thread that runs through it:

"Dum Spiro Spero—while I breathe, I hope."

I believe we should solemnly repent for any ungodly actions that occurred during the time our city was founded. I also believe we must hold on to this redemptive thread, breathe, breathe, take another breath and believe again that we are a city of destiny. No matter our uncertain beginnings we can have a certain hope and a future as we build the Kingdom of God among this land and this people.

CHAPTER THIRTEEN

TIME FOR PREACHING

"To the intent that now unto the principalities and powers in heavenly places MIGHT BE KNOWN BY THE CHURCH the manifold wisdom of God." Ephesians 3:10

Preaching was scarce in the early days of Taney County. In fact, historians Schoolcraft (1818) and Turnbo (1828) both noted the lack of religious exercise among the earliest pioneers. However, as early as 1806 a young Methodist named John Travis was assigned to the Missouri Circuit with the request to form a circuit where he could. The 1807 conference reported from Missouri—two circuits, one hundred white members and six colored.

Speaking of these hardy souls in a short book called, *The Forgotten Man,* the author wrote:

> He began as an itinerant; he continued as an itinerant, he never ceased to be an itinerant. He rode the widest circuit a preacher ever had and served the longest list of appointments. He rode to these appointments in a continuous round; he rode through uncharted wildernesses to the remotest hut of the adventuresome settler; rode in winter's storms and summer's heat, day and night; rode with his saddlebags; rode with his change of garments; rode with his Greek and Hebrew Testaments; rode in the company and

> rode along; rode, rode, rode, till he reeled in the saddle from weariness; rode till sickness halted him; rode till his faithful horse was spent; rode till his final summons came; rode into the jaws of death; rode till the white horse of immortality bore him up out of the black water to his last appointment in glory to be with Christ.

By the time Missouri celebrated statehood, the Missouri Conference was formed and there were five circuits in its bounds including White River. By 1831 the first Southwest Missouri assignment was given to James Slavins. His territory included, Springfield and White River, St. Francois and Saline, a circuit 100 miles north and south by 200 miles east and west.

"My great-grandfather, Reverend David Hadley Pickett, a Methodist minister, was the first to ever preach a gospel sermon in Forsyth," claimed Almeda Brittain in her book, *Pioneer Preacher of the Ozarks.* Methodists generally, however, were not those who lingered to build church structures since their headquarters still viewed the region as a "missionary territory." Saddles must be filled and the next appointment met down the road in another hamlet.

The Baptists appeared in Southwest Missouri as early as 1815. After white settlements were established, they moved into our region and quickly began to establish organized church congregations. Meetings were generally held in the local schoolhouse if one existed and if not, someone's home served as the temple.

The Presbyterians began work in the Ozarks several years after the Baptist and Methodists. The Cumberland Presbyterian Churches organized in the Ozarks several decades after the Methodists and Baptists. In 1848 the presbytery was divided into six circuits of two counties each; Newton and Barry, Dade and Jasper, Taney and Ozark, Greene and Wright, Polk and Dallas, Benton and St. Clair.

Prior to 1882, the General Baptist worked at evangelizing and church planting in Taney County. That year the Missouri Association lettered off four churches for the purpose of making a new association. These churches were Pilgrim's Rest, Antioch, Sardis and Ball Hill. They met in the home of Reverend Cornelius Johnson where they organized the White River Association still active today. By 1883, three more churches had entered the association. Cornelius's son, Brother U.G. Johnson, often called the "Boy Preacher," spent 71 years in the ministry of the gospel. His great compassion for souls won the admiration and respect of all who knew him. Soon he became the most influential preacher of his day. Unfortunately, he saw no conflict in his vigorous presentation of the gospel and his participation in the vigilante hangings of Frank and Tubal Taylor in 1885.

Reverend J.H. Haworth, "Uncle John" of Sardis Church, was converted from a life of sin under the preaching of U. G. Johnson. Forsaking his place as captain on the river while floating rafts of native cedar logs down White River, he became a powerful preacher. He was also an outspoken critic of the Bald Knobbers and active in the Anti-Bald Knobbers.

His uncle, Jordan M. Haworth (Jurd) was also an outspoken critic of the vigilante organization. Jordan was the minister of the Pleasant Hill Christian Church. Unfortunately, he found no conflict between his church activities and that of the Masons. He was a founding member of the Lodge at Forsyth and a Past Worshipful Master since 1877.

The Taney Enterprise noted on Thursday, March 1, 1883, "There is preaching the third Sabbath in every month by Reverend J.M. Beard at Cedar Valley." However, not all preaching was so factually reported. A sarcastic editor wrote in the *Cassville Republican* on February 23, 1899, "We have received from a minister in Eureka Springs an offer to hold a meeting here. Think of it, brethren, a minister offering to preach for us in this time of scarcity! For years we have been left during the winter time to wander in heathen darkness, and only when spring chickens, sweet potatoes, and other luxuries were the bill of fare could we hope for any ray of light."

Nat Kinney, Captain of the notorious Bald Knobbers claimed to be the first to establish a Sunday school in Taney County, but historian Lyn Morrow says residents were attending Sunday schools in both the county and in Springfield as early as 1880.

When the Taylor brothers were dragged from jail and hung from the oak tree, the young deputy on duty was also shot and killed. Three souls entered eternity by violence that dark night. Ingenthron recounts that "allegedly present were Reverends Van Zandt, Power, Spears, Owen, Johnson, Winkle and Smith, three Methodist, two Disciples of Christ and two Baptists."

After the Christian County Bald Knobbers broke into the Edens' home and murdered Edens and Green and injured their wives and children, the sheriff began sweeping the county for the assailants. "As Sheriff Johnson and his posse fanned out to make the initial arrests, Pastor Simmons conducted funerals for William Edens and Charles Green at his Chadwick Baptist Church. The 30-year-old farmer/preacher's baritone voice soared above the congregation's singing. Two days later, the sheriff arrested Pastor Simmons as a murder suspect." At trial he was sentenced to 12 years in the state penitentiary after he pled guilty to second-degree murder (Ingenthron).

Many shameful acts were done by clergy during the violent Bald Knobber years. These actions were called into question, and it was even debated that a well-spring of division in the churches may have been related to this fact. However, in *The General Baptist History,* the author rushed to discount this idea:

> The association in 1953 reported to the General Association with 19 churches, 595 members and 58 ministers. Some heresy has been evidenced among the churches and ministers at various times. Early in its life, White River felt the effect of the Knobbers, an organization made famous in Harold Bell Wright's Shepherd of the Hills. This band of men naturally created unrest and suspicion in the hills but so far as having any direct effect upon the churches, none has been discovered.

Really? Read on.

"Many of the General Baptist churches I pastored had turbulent histories. Certainly Thornfield. And Chadwick, a church which shared with two other denominations a building that had been in existence since the 1800s. Union churches were rather common in rural areas where money and buildings were scarce. I pastored the Chadwick church from 1933 to 1935," wrote Almeda Brittain. This church was the same church in which C.O. Simmons, convicted Bald Knobber murderer, had served as pastor in 1887.

Although there were many spots of shame among area pastors and believers, positive memories were also recorded about how they behaved. Denominations

sometimes shared facilities and helped in services. One reason is because many settlers were harshly abusive toward preachers in general. During camp meetings one minister was usually in charge and remained in residence for the entire period. Several other men of God invariably assisted him during that time. "I've seen as many as 40 or 50 preachers at one of them," said Uncle Joe Cranfield, Kissee Mills. "Every preacher around in the whole country would come. It didn't make any difference about his denominational standing. He was Brother So-and-So.... They left off their denominations. They preached the Bible."

In 1901, a new kind of preacher made his way into the Ozark hills. He came, symbolically enough, in the year of the terrible drought. There was a drought for rain and a drought for preaching the Word of God. The missionary was young Reverend James Forsythe, a recent graduate of the Presbyterian seminary. He became pastor of the Forsyth Presbyterian Church which had been established only five years earlier.

He wrote his parents in mid July, "These are wonderful people, proud, honest, and hard-working without the luxuries of the world and little formal education but they are hospitable and sharing. They seem hungry for the Word of God. And with His help, I will do my best to feed them. I am deeply concerned for their physical welfare too. They raise nearly all of their food and the long, dry spell we are having is ruining their gardens. Drinking water is also a worry. Wells and springs are drying up and most of the streams flow sluggishly if at all. Pastures are burned up so both food and water are problems for the animals. I wish I could do something to help them."

One day in the latter part of August, an elder of the church repeated his requests for rain. “When’s it going to rain, Preacher?”

“In His time brother; God always answers prayer, not necessarily in our way and when we think He should, but in His way and in His time. Trust Him brother, Trust Him. He may test us but He won’t forsake us,” responded young Forsythe.

At 4:30 that afternoon, the sky opened and the first rain in 100 days poured down upon the Ozark Hills. The next edition of *The Republican* noted, “A Thanksgiving service was held at the church to give expression of thanks by song and prayer of gratitude felt for the refreshing showers bestowed upon our land.”

What made Forsythe unique was the fact he became convinced that the young people of this region were capable of further academic exercises, but often without the means to participate. In 1907 Forsythe founded The School of the Ozarks. Here children who “were worthy but without means” could work their way through the school and also “be given Christian instruction which would influence their households for years to come.”

Inspired by his success, in 1908, Dr. Elizabeth McIntyre, the region’s only female doctor, began a campaign to raise money for the first permanent church building in Branson. School children sold blackberries, had pie suppers, and canvassed the town for donations. Henry Sullenger, owner of the saloon was the first contributor. In 1911 when the structure was completed, Sullenger encouraged his children to regularly attend although he declined to do so himself. Years later his son told me that as an eleven-year-old boy Henry began operating gambling tables and games in order to help his family. Later he became a saloon keeper and bootlegger sure that his sin was too great for Christ's blood.

The building produced as a result of Dr. McIntyre's heart for the children of the region was shared by a couple of church denominations until finally the Presbyterians had the use of the facility alone. Today, the remodeled building is used by First Presbyterian Church and stands as a memorial to vision and compassion.

The School of the Ozarks was enjoying its first academic year when another event stirred the communities. The Pentecostal experience came to Taney County. George Youngblood was born in Denver, Arkansas, just below the Taney County line. His father was Powell Youngblood, a half Cherokee Indian whose full blood mother never learned the English language. Powell married Sarah Bethina Potter, an Irish immigrant, the wealthy daughter of an Irish lawyer. Although Sarah Bethina was a cultured lady, her husband Powell and their son George were not. They were rough men who often traveled up the old wagon trail to Pine Top at the State Line Saloon to buy their whiskey.

In early 1905 George was converted at a meeting in Siloam Springs, Arkansas, where an old man by the name of John James brought the gospel. George and his wife Anna Victoria Spohn had moved there shortly after their marriage. John James had been converted and received the baptism of the Holy Ghost in Topeka, Kansas, where Charles Parham first experienced the outpouring of the Holy Spirit. George never meant to get converted. In fact he had never meant to go to one "of those meetings" except that his friends reported that his "half Cherokee father and full Irish mother (a Campellite) had been attending." George went to see what was going on and "felt the power so strong my hair stood on ends."

Afterwards, he shut himself up in the bedroom telling his wife not to bother him because he was going to fast and pray and tarry until he too was filled with this glorious power. He was shut up for three weeks and then wonderfully baptized with the glorious power of the Holy Ghost. Although George had never been taught to read, he was miraculously able to read the Holy Bible. He and his father, traveled into Taney County where they preached in a little church called Cedar Valley. Later in 1907, Powell started a Pentecostal church in Stone County just west of the White River. The church is now called Bowman Pentecostal Church.

In a phone interview with Bonnie Youngblood, she told me a story her father-in-law had related to her about even preachers getting saved. "Old Man Dr. Seals preached for 40 years and had never been saved. After Pentecost came to Siloam Springs, he scoffed in doubt until one night he was sitting on his front porch. He heard his neighbor, Witt, climb a dark hillside and begin to cry out to God for the baptism of the Holy Ghost. When he heard Witt "pray through" he was so moved that the next evening he showed up at the jam-packed church service. There were so many people that he could not get in so he knelt in the doorway and cried out for salvation. Later, he crawled on his knees through the crowd to the altar where he confessed that he'd never experienced salvation until that night although he had preached for 40 years."

During one of the Pentecostal meetings at Cedar Valley, Jim Smythe was converted and filled with the Holy Ghost. Jim was a man of Cherokee descent who married a one-quarter Cherokee woman by the name of Nellie Qualls. Jim brought the message of Pentecost to eastern Taney County at the behest of Lizzie Nave, a local woman who had traveled to see relatives in California where she had been filled with the Holy Ghost on Azusa Street.

Jim preached often in and around the Protem area in the far eastern part of Taney County. A well-circulated story is told about the sanctity of the man's prayer life. "Jim prayed so long and so often on a certain knoll near the cemetery on the creek side that his knees left imprints upon the ground. For years and years afterward, no moss would grow on this section of the knoll although moss grew everywhere else," said Ozarks native B.F. Jennings.

Throughout the teens and twenties of the Twentieth Century tensions began to grow between the Pentecostal believers and members of other church denominations. "Many Baptist and Church of Christ hated the Pentecost," said Jim Groves, grandson of another well-known preacher, John Groves. John Groves suffered thrown eggs, rotten tomatoes and smoke-outs where the mischief makers covered the church chimney with a wet blanket to "smoke out the Holy Rollers." Groves was undaunted. He regularly preached throughout the region. In a 1943 edition of the *National Geographic* he was chronicled as a "self-taught Pentecostal preacher who swept the region with brush arbors and one room school house meetings."

Well-known Branson banker and developer Ben Parnell, whose own mother and grandmother founded the Branson Christian Church, confessed that as a youngster he sometimes attended "Holy Roller" services in the old tobacco barn in Branson for the express purpose of disrupting services and mocking the churchgoers. Tensions escalated further when a well-known Baptist evangelist Bob Grady experienced Pentecost. In the little town of Protem the antagonism between Baptist and Pentecost was stirred by sinners and religious folk alike. According to native B.F. Jennings, "I was just six years old when my brother and I witnessed men pouring kerosene on the Baptist Church." They burned it down and later that same year burned down the Pentecostal church.

Tempers cooled and the two groups began to co-exist more peacefully. Soon both denominations shared the use of the Union Church building for their different services. In fact, in the late 1940's a Baptist preacher by the name of George Shaffer, urged Protem residents to "get on up to church, and if you don't come here at least go down to that Pentecostal church. Go somewheres!" Thank God Jim Smythe spent so many hours laboring in prayer in Protem!

In the meantime, bucking a male-dominated culture, a woman preacher by the name of Almeda Brittain was traveling through the county preaching the gospel "every time I was asked." When she was just three months old, her great-granddaddy Reverend David Hadley Pickett had laid his hands on her as he lay on his deathbed and cried, "God, take this child and use her for the salvation of many souls!" God did. In 1924, Almeda preached her first sermon at St. James General Baptist Church near Kirbyville and from then on was a frequent revivalist. She pastored several different churches. For several years, she served as pastor for three different churches at the same time.

Formal schooling for preachers was scarce. Almeda remembered, "The revival was in its midst when I was contacted to come home to attend a Bible school for preachers at Forsyth. The church at Ava consented for me to leave and return in the fall to finish the revival. I was so happy for the summons and for the understanding of the church members, for I have always tried to learn all I could about the Bible. The Reverend George E. Gray of the Moody Bible Institute taught the school. The Reverend U.G. Johnson was one of those at Dr. Gray's course. He told the rest of us that we were learning things it took him 40 years to figure out for himself."

She recounted a revival in Bradleyville. "There I stood for fourteen nights straight, preaching under the anointing of the Holy Spirit until it seemed that all the saints of God were singing—but not a move was made by the unsaved. Finally, on the fifteenth night when I gave the altar call, penitents came faster than I could find places for them. Down on our knees we went to pray and one after another was saved."

I'm ready for a great awakening like this multiplied times thousands that fills the altars of every church with penitents weeping over their sins and running into the arms of their sweet Savior. The Apostle Paul wrote:

> (Whereof) I was made a minister, according to the gift of the grace of God given unto me by the effectual working of his power. Unto me, who am less than the least of all saints, is this grace given, that I should preach among the Gentiles the unsearchable riches of Christ; and to make all men see what is the fellowship of the mystery, which from the beginning of the world hath been hid in God, who created all things by Jesus Christ: to the intent that now unto the principalities and powers in heavenly places might be known by the church the manifold wisdom of God (Ephesians 3:7-10).

If I understand this passage correctly, Paul was saying that the manifold (multi-faceted, many-dimensional) wisdom of God is meant to be displayed through the Body of Christ to principalities and powers. The thought here is that this display of the power and glory of God through us is meant to defeat the foe.

I rejoice that the glorious Gospel of Jesus Christ has been preached throughout this region for generations. Although it is true the preachers "saw through a glass darkly" and sometimes walked without much scriptural revelation, still Jesus Christ has been preached. However, I am longing for the day we are so cleansed and free from the influence of superstitions, revenge, greed, supremacy, and religious rituals that the full measure of Christ can be displayed to the lost through us. The measure of power we have against principalities is directly related to the measure of truth in which we walk. May the true Believers of this land walk in absolute truth so that we may have absolute victory!

CHAPTER FOURTEEN

RACIAL SUPREMACY

"I opened the door of my heart to the people of another race and color of skin. Outside the influence of Christ in my life, it has proven to be the most enriching experience." E. Stanley Jones

Personal Journal
May 21, 2002

This morning I woke up knowing:
"...that Roger B. Taney, (for whom our county was named) rendered the decision that became known as the Dred Scott Decision." I heard the Holy Spirit refer to him as "one of the most racist men ever." I began to research this man and discovered that he made harsh racial comments calling Blacks "unfit to live as citizens of the United States." I was alarmed that our forefathers had been inspired to name our county for such a man. I knew the Holy Spirit was drawing my attention to another aspect of our colored history.

Interestingly, I had not been studying anything remotely pertaining to Roger B. Taney or the Dred Scott decision and to my knowledge had never even read any part of the Dred Scott decision. I do think I vaguely remember knowing that Taney was the one who rendered the decision and that he was our county's namesake. But I was startled to wake up hearing the phrase, "one of the most racist men ever...."

In 1857, the *Dred Scott Case* was decided by the United States Supreme Court. This ruling declared a federal law that prohibited slavery in American territories outside the South to be unconstitutional. This act reaffirmed the "race exception" and explicitly added racism to our Constitution. If the Supreme Court was right, then the Constitution prohibited Congress from abolishing slavery where it existed and where it did not exist. The opinion written by Chief Justice Roger B. Taney was motivated by his own views of racial supremacy. Taney wrote "Blacks are subordinate and inferior beings who had been subjugated by the dominant race, and, whether emancipated or not, yet remained subject to their authority." His opinion included not only slaves, but all Blacks throughout the United States. According to Taney, the Constitution permanently excluded Blacks from national citizenship and established them legally as less than fully human, as "subordinate and inferior beings." According to Chief Taney, "Blacks had no rights which the white man was bound to respect."

I became concerned that our county was named for a man such as this. To me it was bad enough that our first people, the Osage, held beliefs of their racial supremacy. It was tragic to have this more or less affirmed by the people who named our county. Racial prejudice was alive and well in the Ozarks and unfortunately still is.

I do not believe racial prejudice and racial supremacy has its roots in slavery although slavery did exist in our region. Our first people, the Osage, took enemy survivors as slaves. Wealthier Cherokee often had black slaves. In fact, there is a division of tribal membership for Cherokee Freedmen, descendants of those slaves. Some early settlers owned slaves which were most likely considered "family slaves." The 1850 slave schedule of Taney County lists 99 slaves. The 1860 schedule lists 82. J. Vaughn appeared to be the largest slave owner with 15 slaves consisting of what probably included three slave families. Jack, a slave freed by Hank Snapp was sent to live at a spring and care for the Snapp family's range cattle. The spring came to be known as Free Jack Spring. It is still located on the Strahan's land down J Highway south of Kirbyville, MO.

In *Stories of the Pioneers,* Uncle Ben McKinney said, "Father had six slaves when the war broke out. There were a number of families near Forsyth and on Swan Creek and Beaver that had slaves. Very few of these slaves were profitable, but some of them were very good." Since slavery in Taney County was not prolific, nor profitable, I believe prejudice and supremacy was motivated by something other than that. I believe racial prejudice and supremacy was and still is rooted in ignorance and the damning pride it so often accommodates. People naturally fear that which is different from them. People naturally believe they are superior to someone else. And, of course, to be superior there always has to be an inferior.

"The end of the Rebellion had not brought the complete end of southern resistance. To combat some of the evils of the victor-imposed carpetbag government, the Ku Klux Klan was organized. It was primarily an anti-Negro organization, designed to control the newly freed blacks and their northern friends. The Klan flourished best where the Negro population was greatest. In the borderlands of Missouri and Arkansas, where there were few Negroes, there was little Klan activity" (Ingenthron).

Ingenthron may have been too optimistic when he penned those lines. Even in the region where the Black population was sparse, mob activity could still be found. In 1906 in Springfield, Missouri, four black men were hung on the square.

In 1921, a Nazi swastika was flying from the upper window of the McGill building in Branson. Why? A relative newcomer to the area was publishing from the second story of the building, a violent and arrogant newspaper called *The New Menace.* Billy Parker, President of The New Menace Publishing Company, was owner and editor of this "hate" newspaper which targeted Jews, Catholics, Blacks, foreigners and anarchists. Parker was also a single-minded lecturer, encouraging "healthy, virile Americanism." Many of his meetings were held under the auspices of the Klan. Articles published in *The New Menace* cast suspicions on the Catholics and Jews, denigrated Blacks and accused the government of betraying its citizens. One issue discussed a case in Houston, Texas, where the Masonic Order, Odd Fellows, and the Ku Klux Klan were being brought into question concerning the flogging of Mrs. R. H. Harrison and R. A. Armand of Goose Creek oil field. The article accused the "Knights of Columbus grand jury" for bringing the charges.

The newspaper, published until 1931, headquartered in Kansas City, was also published in Aurora, MO. For reasons unknown to us, Parker's divisive enterprise didn't thrive in Branson. In 1922, *The New Menace* announced it was leaving Branson to return to Aurora, its original home. According to the authors of *Hometown Branson,* that same summer the Ku Klux Klan announced it had organized a Branson group and claimed 100 members in this area.

Before he died, Art Cahill, a 95-year-old resident of Branson told me, "There was a certain group of young bucks who would threaten any Blacks who tried to get off the train in Branson. They would go up to the Black and say, 'Do you know so-and-so?' When the Black would say, No, I don't know him. The group would laugh and say, 'Well, he got off the train a few days ago and hasn't been seen since.' Of course, the Black would turn around and get back on the train."

Hollister was figuring prominently in the racist activity as well. Hollister historian Viola Hartman wrote in *The Ghost of Gobbler's Knob and Other Tales of the Hill Country,* "There were other things, less factual perhaps, that puzzled and intrigued me—one being the Sundown Law. While no one seemed to have a clear knowledge of its origin, the meaning was broadly hinted. Considering the troubles of the time and place, it was possible such a thing existed; yet no one could verify that it had been more than a lot of other stories blown out of proportion. I inquired of several members of the law enforcement and legal branches of the local government without success. None of the young men I talked with had any knowledge of such a law.

"The law," had no official status. It was simply the law of the land and stated that any Blacks traveling through the country must be gone from the community by sundown. Moreover, for a time a sign placed at the Hollister railroad station read:

No Negro shall set foot on this town's soil!

"It wasn't bigotry, at least in our little town. Although I'm sure the people were going along with the general code of the hill country. You must understand—there was very little employment then and any outsiders who came in to work took what we considered our livelihood," one native reasoned in Hartman's book.

Flying in the face of established beliefs, Branson banker Ben Parnell did his part to break down racial barriers in the 1960s when he hired a Black couple to attend to his family's houseboat and prepare the meals when he entertained area businessmen. The whispers were somewhat muted by the enormous regard the community held for the Parnell family. One of Ben's grandfathers was Sheriff McHaffie, one of the thirteen original Baldknobbers who withdrew from the vigilantes after the violent hanging of the Taylor brothers. Ben was also the son of B. Albert Parnell, the much-loved pioneer of the Branson business community and former multi-term mayor. Ben himself was one of the men responsible for gaining Congressional approval for the funding of the Table Rock Dam which created Table Rock Lake and millions of dollars worth of tourism revenues.

One might erroneously believe that racist views do not exist in our modern times. However, I have an eye witness testimony to the contrary and scores of reports from various watchdog groups, media and the racists themselves.

In the late 1980s, a Branson businessman was invited to lunch with two well-known community figures. During the discussion, several references were made that caused the businessman to know his hosts held a dangerous, racist point of view. Later, he was given a packet of information containing "hate" literature which his wife promptly destroyed.

A "pure race" group known as *Songs for His People* sponsors an annual "Winter Fest" in Branson usually attended by a few hundred people who share their "Christian Identity" viewpoints. They bring in some of the top speakers in the Christian Identity movement of today including Ted Weiland and Pete Peters. The essence of the group's teachings is that the "true" children of Israel are the people who trace their ancestral roots to the white, European and Saxon (Germanic) peoples. They believe the Jews to be imposters and certainly not heirs to the promises of Abraham, which they claim for themselves.

The Center for New Community, a watchdog group that tracks racist activities posted on their website in February 2001: "Some of the most infamous white supremacists in the United States plan on returning to the Midwest over Memorial Day weekend. The LaPorte, Colorado-based Scriptures for America (Pete Peters) will hold its 'Big Branson Memorial Day Rally' at the Chateau on the Lake, May 25-27, 2001. (The Chateau later cancelled the contract and the event was held at Settle Inn instead.)

The annual "rally" is hosted by Scriptures for America leader, Pete Peters, the country's leading exponent of the racist and anti-Semitic pseudo-theology of "Christian Identity." The event, which melds "fine dining and Christian fellowship" with hardcore racist strategizing, features speeches by leading preachers of hate including Earl Jones, Charles Weisman and Peters. The claims that there will be no "hate-oriented" activities at the event seem disingenuous, given the list of scheduled speakers. Weisman voices support of genocide of the Jewish people and for a United States comprised of only "white people." Jones wants a "Culture War" to "defend European White Culture." In addition, Peters claims the Bible calls for the "execution of gays and lesbians."

All of them share the pure race and anti-Semitic theology of the "Christian Identity Movement." Also known as "Israel Identity," "Christian Israel" or "Racial

Identity," the religion teaches that white Europeans and descendants of white Europeans are the Biblical "chosen people." Extremists believe that Jews are the literal "seed of Satan" and people of color are "subhuman."

According to the watchdog group, Center for New Community, the appearance of Peters in our area was significant because his meetings were an obvious effort to discover whether or not he could "mobilize a significant number of believers and establish a permanent base of bigotry in the region."

I have numerous newspaper and magazine clippings of articles published about these groups meeting in Branson. The F.B.I. keeps a close watch on seventeen supremacist "churches" in Southwest Missouri alone. One of these churches is pastored by Thom Robb, the national director of the Knights of the Ku Klux Klan who lives just outside Harrison, Arkansas.

Just a mile from my house is a one lane, dirt road that leads deep into the woods to a high-fenced compound covered with signs warning "government intruders will be shot." Confederate flags and swastikas decorate the fence.

Last month my husband and brother were doing business with a man who also holds an elected state office. He said he wasn't going to watch a certain television show until they stopped showing so many Blacks. After he left the counter to retrieve something, my brother looked at my husband and asked, "Is he racist?" Apparently he is because he reiterated that line of thinking again later. Neither my husband nor brother entered into the spirit of his conversation, so he fell silent.

Racial supremacy and racial prejudice is still alive and well in the Ozarks. However, over the past 10 years there has been a major increase of people of color choosing to make this land their home too. The science of

DNA has proven the human genome structure varies exactly the same percentage no matter the amount of pigment a person has in his or her skin. "DNA studies do not indicate that separate classifiable subspecies (races) exist within modern humans. While different genes for physical traits such as skin and hair color can be identified between individuals, no consistent patterns of genes across the human genome exist to distinguish one race from another. There also is no genetic basis for divisions of human ethnicity" (Human Genome Project).

In his book, *Victorious Living*, published in 1934, Methodist missionary and theologian, E. Stanley Jones called racial prejudice "self-starvation." While serving as a missionary to Africa, one day Jones offered his seat on a street car to a Negro woman. "I heard a titter run through the crowd behind me. 'He doesn't know what he's let himself in for!' Hence the laugh. But the laugh is now on the other side. I opened the door of my heart to the people of another race and color of skin. Outside the influence of Christ in my life, it has proven to be the most enriching experience. What love, what friendships, what wisdom, what Christlikeness, what nobility have come to me during these years through that open door! The people on the street car that day closed their door with a bang of superiority, but they starved themselves."

The Apostle Paul wrote in Galatians 3:28, "There is neither Jew nor Greek, there is neither bond nor free, there is neither male nor female: for ye are all one in Christ Jesus." To supremacists and the racially prejudice, I say there are only two races—the human race and the race that is set before you. The sooner we accept the former the better off we will run the latter.

CHAPTER FIFTEEN

WITCHCRAFT

"The longer we choose to be spectators and not participants in this war, the more we play into Satan's hands. The only way to put an end to the various witchcrafts is with the power of the gospel of Jesus Christ."
Pablo Bottari

My first encounter with the occult was in 1996 when a woman I had been doing business with stood in front of my office desk and during a horrific verbal assault called me names I've never heard before. *Suddenly she flew from in front of me to the end of the office and back.* When she abruptly left my office, I crawled under my desk and trembled violently until my husband came during lunch hour to find me. My body literally had gone into shock. I found it nearly impossible to speak. Concerned and unable to determine what had happened, my husband called our pastor who came and prayed with me. It was weeks before I could comprehend what had happened and nearly two years before I ever spoke of it to anyone.

Six months after her stunning manifestation, I had lost my business and withdrew from the business community. I cried unto God in hours upon hours of tearful agony, begging that He would never let me feel that terrified or powerless again. Out of that desperate intercession came the impetus and direction to research our spiritual history. I was looking for clues to help me understand what I had encountered. Who was that woman really, and why was she able to do that?

One day in prayer and intercession I heard the Lord say, "principality." Immediately He brought to my mind the faces of two people I knew well. One was the woman who had flown from one end of my office to the other. The other person I saw was her husband. Then the Lord said, "High priest and high priestess." I was absolutely floored. This couple was well-known in the community. In fact, at that time the husband had a very important position in our government.

Human Sacrifice

I was forced to consider the unsavory truth that our community had a dark underbelly. I remembered that in 1987 my husband had attended a police training school. During the week, he made the acquaintance of another officer from St. Charles, Missouri, who was on the squad that investigated the activities of the occult. He made the comment to Steve, "Boy, you have a lot of activity going on in Branson!" Steve was surprised and asked the officer what he meant. He proceeded to tell him about the occult activity they had investigated that led to Branson and had even indicated human sacrifice. In one investigation they followed a young teenaged girl who had been impregnated in the occult. Later when she was due, she was sent to Branson. According to the officer, "she was pregnant when she left but not when she returned and she never brought back a baby with her."

In 1996, we came across considerable evidence that three major active covens were at work in this region. The same leadership rules all three groups, and, by the way, is also active in the Christian Identity Movement and the regional drug trade.

In 1997, a young woman burst into the doors of a local church screaming for help. She began to manifest demonically. The pastor and his wife, along with two staff members, cast the demons out of the girl. After she was in her right mind and able to speak, she explained that she had gotten involved with her boyfriend in a coven "down near Blue Eye." She reported that she had overheard a conversation that she was to be the next sacrifice for the coven. In terror, she called her mother who lived in another state and told her what was intended. Her mother urged her to go to a church and ask for help. She remembered the church she passed everyday as she traveled back and forth from Branson to Blue Eye. There that young woman gave her heart to Jesus Christ. She was given safe shelter by another woman in the church who helped her grow in the knowledge of the Lord Jesus Christ. I met and ministered to her personally a few times. She was later married. The last I heard, she and her husband were serving as youth pastors in the Kansas City area.

During my research, an internet website caught my attention: "Portal of Light is a bunch of people who come together for ritual, to celebrate the Sabbats, to support each other, and has expanded rapidly to include people in Branson, Ft. Smith, Lebanon, Warrensburg, Columbia and other places unknown." In 2000 and 2001 there was a wave of interest in Wicca which flooded the area.

Springfield police officers were well aware of satanic activities in certain parts of the city especially during the early and mid 1990s. One retired police officer personally told me of several sites he regularly patrolled to investigate the latest in animal sacrifices. He also spoke about depraved persons who dug up gravesites in order to strip the dead bodies of jewelry and gold teeth. One perpetrator taunted police by scattering the bones of these bodies around different areas of the city and using them in sorceries.

The kingdom of darkness operates in darkness because according to the scriptures "their deeds are evil." These evil deeds can range from human sacrifice to cursing churches with spells so powerful congregants destroy each other and the church for reasons they cannot even remember years later. Satanists specialize in casting spells that produce untimely deaths, multiple catastrophes, and cycles of tragedies in their victim's lives. Other Satanists perpetrate evil and finance the growth of evil by managing prostitution rings, producing pornography and especially child pornography, and tightly controlling the drug trade. Mysterious disappearances are often connected to the covens.

The Witches' Brew

For years, the scourge of drug abuse in the region included alcohol, and in the early days, moonshine. In the 60s and 70s marijuana became popular and easy to grow and hide in the wild lands of the Ozark Mountains. In fact, it still is. Sadly, drug use and abuse have been generational here in our region. In the late 1980s, however, it got far worse ironically at the same time the leader of the local coven traveled to California. He brought back two things; a high priestess, an even more dangerous witch than himself, and he opened the channels of commerce for the most potent form of witchcraft--methamphetamine.

I am connecting witchcraft to the scourge of methamphetamine because of the word "sorceries." In the Greek, the word *sorceries* is translated *pharmakeia.* Strong's Concordance says this is used of medicine, drugs, or spells and later the word was used of poisoning, and then of sorcery, accompanied by drugs, incantations, charms, and magic.

Picture the witches of Endor concocting a noxious brew of toxic chemicals from which a look-a-like spirit of Samuel appears to King Saul. Consider Shakespeare's scene in Macbeth where the three witches conjure from a boiling pot a spirit to advise the king. Fast forward to the reality of today's Ozark Mountains. Methamphetamine "cooks" are busy brewing a destructive sorcery that has swept the country into a cauldron of pain and misery.

Methamphetamine, often called meth, crank, crystal, Tina, poor man's cocaine, or horse, was first created by a Japanese chemist in 1919. The Nazis perfected the recipe and made it and their production methods available to their soldiers. Nazi soldiers could hike longer, carry more and stay awake for days at a time. Hitler was an addict.

In the 1980s, Mexican drug cartels began flooding California and surrounding states with the toxic poison. Biker gangs transported the drug across America in their crankshafts, hence the nickname "crank" used for the drug. Bikers also largely controlled distribution through the mid-west.

However, in 1994, a pivotal event occurred. A Springfield, Missouri, resident named Bob Paillet was looking for a way to make a more potent, more cheaply and easily available version of the drug. He found a dusty document in the Springfield library, stamped with a swastika that contained the ephedrine based recipe. The chemical process was easier than the lab method and designed by Nazi scientists in an effort to make the drug more readily available to soldiers in the field. Paillet's potion was 4-6 times stronger than what had been produced in the 1980s. It produced a powerful, instantaneous high.

Today, meth abuse transcends all socio-economic barriers although it is most popular with blue collar, white men and women. The average meth user is not a teenager but in fact, more likely to be his or her parents. Meth floods the brain with dopamine, the "feel good" chemical, capturing and addicting with the first hit. Perceived effects are increased energy, increased heart rate, and feelings of euphoria, decreased inhibitions, increased tolerance to pain, and the ability to stay awake for days at a time. Users have an unnatural appetite for sex, the more sex the better and the more unnatural the sex, the better. They have little to no appetite for food.

Local law enforcement agents can tell you the trade-mark meth house has an almost empty refrigerator, unnatural filth and trash in and around the home, stores of pornography, and if there are children in the home, they mostly likely have been victims of vile sexual abuse.

One meth addict sold her twelve and thirteen-year-old daughters for sex with dealers to get her next hit. Another addict nightly took his live-in girlfriend's nine year old boy out of bed and injected him in the thigh with a needle that "made him feel funny." Then, he was raped. The horror was discovered when a teacher reported he "had trouble sitting down." Another meth addict shot off the head of his sixteen year-old girlfriend "because the devil was coming out of her head."

Brain scans now reveal that the neurons responsible for producing the brain chemistry that processes mood, emotion and nurturing are nearly destroyed after the first or second hit. Mothers and fathers who use this drug lose the natural compassion that causes them to nurture and protect their children. Children subjected to toxic chemicals used during the production of meth develop learning disabilities, disaffective behaviors, violent outbursts, and deep depression. Local schools are being flooded with the sad fall-out of this drug. Children whose brains have already been damaged are boarding school buses, sitting in classrooms and expected to learn while the neurons in their brains have already been woefully damaged.

Meth is the most highly addictive drug available today. Eighty-five percent of users are immediate and long-term addicts. Meth enters the brain more rapidly than other drugs due to the fact that it is water soluble, and the brain is largely made up of water. The repeated release of high volumes of dopamine destroys brain synapses and causes brain damage. Brain scans show a decrease in N-acetylaspartate in the brain's frontal white matter, which is linked to Alzheimer's disease, stroke, epilepsy and Parkinson's disease.

Long term effects for users include skin disorders, organ damage, severe tooth decay, hair damage, severe weight loss, paranoia and brain damage. Users "see" creatures, demonic beings, experience demon attacks and may "feel" bugs crawling on their skin. Users may become assaultive, irrational, and abusive, crave unnaturally rough sex or commit suicide. Taney County Sheriff Jimmy Russell told me, "This doesn't even include the sad fact that nursing homes will soon be flooded with 50-60-year-olds whose minds and bodies have been destroyed."

Law enforcement officials acknowledge the fall-out from meth is incomprehensible. Every week children are being removed from their homes because of this sorcery. In Taney County, *in one day*, eleven cases of child abuse and neglect were recorded. In fact, from 1997-2001 Taney County recorded a jaw-dropping 377% increase in child abuse and neglect.

Meth cooks dot the landscape of the Ozarks with their shoddily built labs. Meth can be cooked in a motel room, pickup truck, apartment or shack in the woods with readily available precursors. Meth cooks enjoy the power rush of combining potentially explosive, toxic chemicals and being "a popular guy." Demonic activity goes hand in hand with meth which addicts often call the "devil's drug," "witches brew," and the "devil in my head."

Where meth appears, burglary immediately increases because the addict can not honestly earn the funds necessary to feed their habit for long. Check kiting, employee pilfering, theft, and shoplifting earmark an addict's life.

Law enforcement agencies across the U.S. are scrambling to keep up with this devastating tornado of witchcraft. Missouri is still the number one state for meth lab seizures with 1,612 in 2010 up from 1,284 in 2006. The state with the next highest number of seizures is Tennessee with 1,084. Taney County had nine seizures in 2006 and six in 2010. Jefferson County had the highest number of seizures with 211 in 2006 and 187 in 2010.

Although Missouri is still the number one state for meth lab seizures, it is not the number one producer of methamphetamine. Currently, Mexican drug cartels are responsible for the production and distribution of the largest volume of this poison. Mexican meth is much more expensive, but improved production methods have created a drug that can be 98% pure and many times more potent. Most independent meth makers create a drug that is only 20-30% pure. Since the middle of the past decade, Mexican drug suppliers have slowly increased their control of drug distribution in our region. This has produced a dangerous demarcation line between local drug producers and distributors and the growing influence of the cartel whose goal is to eventually control all drug production and distribution in the heartland.

Ironically, one of the reasons the cartel has been able to make headway with their plan is that in July 2005, Missouri lawmakers signed into law the *Pseudoephedrine Control Act.* This well-meaning act has decreased the ability of independent meth cooks to access pseudoephedrine, a vital ingredient in the toxic brew. A temporary drop in production created the opportunity for Mexican suppliers to fill the void and increase their network of control.

The witches' brew has certainly done more to bring Ozarkers into captivity than any other single strategy of the enemy. Recovering addicts struggle with the frustration that their brains, outside of a miracle from God, will never fully recover. They struggle to feel basic emotions like happiness, sorrow, compassion or love. Their memory is like a sieve. Their ability to learn is forever harnessed by neurological damage. The few who find their way free from the iron bars of addiction may now be sitting in the church pews awaiting the ministry of healing and deliverance. "I know I need deliverance," one addict told me. "I let the demons in, but now I want them out."

Winter's Bone, a recent Oscar contender and winner of the 2010 Sundance Grand Jury Prize, is an authentic glimpse into the lives of the meth culture in the Ozarks. It reveals the harsh underbelly of this land and the tragic consequences for those human lives trapped in its death grip. Area meth addicts and cooks were uncomfortably uncovered by the story line in the movie, an all-too-familiar storyline. However, it is a movie the Church needs to see. Winter's Bone takes us to the middle of a putrid pond and confronts our lily-white notions with the harsh reality. Lives are being dismembered by meth. We must not close our eyes and pretend we are in a land of milk and honey.

One former meth user aptly called the drug "the white horse conqueror." One hit and the user does an about-face toward destruction while dragging many innocent lives behind them. We need a break-through on this particular form of witchcraft. After that we are going to need thousands of miracles and healings to see lives restored. My heart is so often broken over this witchcraft. I know the horrible face of meth because people who are so dear to me have been so horribly damaged by it.

Sorceries that involve the production and sale of this drug and other drugs is perhaps the most common way the coven manifests its power in the region. It is a deadly power and those who wield it are as serious as death. With the coven, life is meaningless. Power is all-powerful.

Every community has their fair share of "dabblers," those who play at witchcraft and magic. Sadly however, most communities have more than their fair share of serious witches and warlocks who attempt to destroy unsuspecting victims as well as unsuspecting churches with powerful works of dark arts. Pretending the devil and his servants do not exist does not make them disappear. Just as sorcerers existed in the days of King Saul and much later the Apostle Paul so they exist today. No amount of pretending can make them go away.

I want this principality defeated. I want coven leadership in our region to be so radically saved and delivered that witchcraft and all its potions become powerless in the presence of God. I want healing lines for former meth users. I want healing lines for tiny children whose lives have been destroyed by this witches' brew. I want a complete dismantling of the power of the coven. I want everything that has been done in darkness to be brought into the light. I want a victory in Jesus' name for my land and my people, and I know you do too.

CHAPTER SIXTEEN

PYTHON

"When we took authority over this principality in the name of Jesus, two things happened. First, our growth accelerated. Secondly, 40% of all the people we baptized from that time on were neighbors from the city of Androgue itself--instead of neighboring cities as was their history.

Eduardo Lorenzo

Personal Journal
June 1998

"While in prayer today, I suddenly saw a vivid vision of a bull's eye ahead of me with a very clear, red center circle. As I watched, the Lord spoke, 'Time to take down the principality'" Immediately, an arrow zipped passed my ear and struck the target. Bull's eye!"

I sought the Lord carefully all that month and part of the next. Then, a prophet from Memphis, Tennessee, spoke at our church. During one of his messages he taught on the "spirit of python." I listened carefully asking God in my heart if *this* was the principality over our region. Suddenly, during his message the prophet said, "This principality has been ruling here for years."

In August of 1998 however, I received a cassette tape of a message another prophet had given during his visit to Branson in July 1998. In the message, he said that the principality that ruled over Branson was "spirit of divination." I was confused. Both men were clearly accurate and anointed prophetic voices, both messages came to me *after* I had received the vision and heard the Lord say, "time to take down the principality!" But they appeared to be giving conflicting messages.

For two years I was perplexed. However, I continued my research. Finally, in the year 2,000, while studying the scriptures I was transfixed by the passage in Acts 16 where the damsel "possessed with a spirit of divination" vexed Paul and Silas by crying out "these are the servants of the Most High God." In the margin of the reference Bible I was studying at the time, I was excited to see that this "spirit of divination" was indeed Python.

That same year, I received this dream:

> I was going through a cave that contained a series of "honeycombs." The passageways were often so narrow that the rough walls of the cave scraped my skin off as I struggled through. I could hear a distinct rumbling sound in the distance. As I got closer, the sound became more like a roar. This tunnel concluded into a very large cave room from which this now thunderous roar had been coming. All around the room, lying upon the floor were many, many men and women in loud and continuous intercessory prayer. The cave room was filled with a golden haze.
>
> I looked toward what appeared to be the front of the room. There was a table covered with maps and papers where I stood seemingly giving out information to different intercessors.
>
> Immediately, I was taken atop ground. I was standing on a gentle slope before a great valley, which was terribly dry and destitute of grass and trees. Out of the right side of my vision our pastor came striding purposefully

toward an object off in the distance. I couldn't tell what this object was so I headed off after Pastor. As we got closer, I could see the object was a gigantic snake. The body was as thick as we were tall. He strode up to the snake, which was wrapped protectively around something which I could not see. The head of the snake suddenly rose up in a threatening gesture and as it did, it appeared as the head of Jezebel with huge painted eyelids and a very seductive look. Its head whipped around again and suddenly it had the head of a Pharisee, with the headgear like I had seen in The Promise music show. A third time the head whipped around into my face but I could not see its image.

Suddenly, Pastor produced a giant sword with which, taking only one stroke, he lopped off the head of the snake. The snake instantly uncoiled from the object and then disintegrated He stepped up to what I could now see was a large, flat rock. He bent down and began to struggle to work this rock back and forth. Men appeared and together they wrested this flat rock off and up bubbled an amazing spring. The spring began to flow down the valley and as I watched the stream grow, the entire valley turned a vibrant green. Lush grass and beautiful trees filled the valley as far as the eye could see. Then my dream ended.

During my prayer time I was led to study the passage in Acts 16:16-19:

Now it happened, as we went to prayer, that a certain slave girl possessed with a spirit of divination met us, who brought her masters much profit by fortune-telling. This girl followed Paul and us, and cried out, saying, "These men are the servants of the Most High God, who proclaim to us the way of salvation." And this she did for many days. But Paul, greatly annoyed, turned and said to the spirit, "I command you in the name of Jesus Christ to come out of her." And he came out that very hour. But when her masters saw that their hope of profit was gone, they seized Paul and Silas and dragged them into the marketplace to the authorities.

According to *Dake Annotated Reference Bible*, this spirit of divination was the spirit of python, or Apollo. Pytho was, according to Greek legend, a huge serpent that had an oracle on Mt. Parnassus and was famous for predicting future events. Apollo slew this serpent and was called Pythius becoming celebrated as the foreteller of events. It was believed that all who pretended to foretell events were influenced by the spirit of Apollo Pythius. A priestess at his temple was called Pythoness. Through her, messages were delivered.

Python is also referred to as the Spirit of divination. Divination is the art of obtaining secret knowledge, especially of the future. It is the pagan counterpart to prophecy.

Careful comparisons of scripture will reveal that inspirational divination is by demonic power, whereas genuine prophecy is by the Spirit of God. The biblical attitude toward divination is distinctly hostile. In Deuteronomy 18: 10-12, the prophet of Jehovah is contrasted with diviners of all sorts and is set forth as the only authorized medium of supernatural revelation.

God made Himself perfectly clear in Deuteronomy 18:10, "There shall not be found among you any one that maketh his son or his daughter to pass through the fire, or that useth divination, or an observer of the times, or an enchanter, or a witch." This spirit of python is the inspiration (source) of witchcraft and divination.

The Pagan Oracle of Delphi was located about 75 miles NW of Athens on the Corinthian Sea, 5 miles inland and 10 miles south of Mount Parnassos' (Parnassus) summit. There on the sharp, Parnassus Mountain cliffs, at nearly 1900 feet above the Corinthian Gulf, where the sacred spring, Castalia, flows into the Cephissus River, two spectacular crags form a ledge. There the pagan temple of Apollo was located. Steps at one corner reached the lower level of the Temple, and it is said that intoxicating fumes rose from a cleft in the floor near the center of the chamber. These fumes were believed to be the smell from the decaying python, which Apollo is said to have killed.

Centuries before the birth of Christ, devout pilgrims made the arduous trek to Delphi to ask for advice from the famous oracle. City-states made generous contributions, some even establishing treasuries on the site. For more than six centuries, until the Christian emperor Arcadius in 398 A.D. destroyed the shrine, Delphi truly shaped the history of the world.

Tradition has it that Delphi was found by Coretas, a shepherd boy, who discovered that his sheep and goats acted strangely when they approached the area and he soon began uttering prophetic statements which came true. However, the priestesses of Daphoene gave oracle at Delphi during Cretan times, which were at least 200 years and possibly 400 years before Apollo. The shepherd, Coretas, obviously did not discover the sight, but rather he uncovered the secret to the priestesses of the Serpent

Oracles of Mother goddess who presided there. Christian sources assert that the priestess at Delphi (Pythoness) was intoxicated by fumes escaping from the underground cavern and that she spoke gibberish which had to be interpreted by the priest, and further that the questions had to be formed so as to receive a "yes" or "no" answer.

People came from all over the world to receive direction and revelation. The priestess (Pythian) would breath in these fumes that came up from the ground which some even called the “prophetic spirit of Apollo” to receive their secret knowledge. Women priestesses would be possessed much like a medium today, and some say that without control and even in a trance state, speak. The people truly believed that the god, Apollo, spoke through the Oracle merely using her vocal cords to express his wishes and advice. Witchcraft (divination) was founded on python worship. This snake was worshipped for thousands of years before Apollo established his famous oracle and temple and was the very symbol of this region.

One other interesting note about the Greek god, Apollo, (which we know is a demon that expressed itself as many other strongholds in ancient mythology) is that he was also known as the god of healing diseases. It is very interesting that even today the natural symbol of medical healing is a serpent and even in Numbers 21 when sickness struck the Israelites, it came with serpents and when God instructed Moses about the remedy, it was a bronze serpent on a pole. Although in ancient Egypt and still places today the most commonly worshipped snake is a cobra, there is a connection between infirmity and the spirit of Python.

The spirit of python works with the spirit of Jezebel. Jezebel not only uses witchcraft, but also promotes and sets a platform for the false prophets of Baal and witchcraft in the land. This spirit serves the agenda of Jezebel and is the source of all-demonic divination and witchcraft.

Deuteronomy 18:11-14 says, "...or a charmer, or a consulter with familiar spirits, or a wizard, or a necromancer. For all that do these things are an abomination unto the LORD: and because of these abominations the LORD thy God doth drive them out from before thee. Thou shalt be perfect with the LORD thy God. For these nations, which thou shalt possess, hearkened unto observers of times, and unto diviners: but as for thee, the LORD thy God hath not suffered thee so to do." God is the true source of revelation, and He does not tolerate imposters.

Python Is After Breath

To better understand how this python spirit attacks believers and the church today, we need to understand some physical facts about this snake before it is brought into a more spiritual understanding.

Python - A genus of very large, nonpoisonous snakes of Burma, Indo-China, India, Mexico, Asia, Africa, the tropics and beyond. These snakes are known to crush their prey to death and kill by suffocation.

There are several different types of pythons and some of these larger pythons are often confused with the boas. Its various species are found throughout the tropics of the world. Some have been reported to be 30 feet or more and weigh 200-250 pounds. Adults are typically between 15 and 20 feet long. Size and weight will vary according to the geographic location in which the python is found.

When the python attacks, one or more coils of the body are thrown around the victim, following up the stroke of the head, and the powerful body muscles apply pressure. The pressure exerted by a large python must be terrific. Killing of the prey happens by constriction and suffocation rather than by any actual crushing of the ribs.

When a python has the victim in its grip, each time he breathes the grip tightens. The death process for the victim is slow and terrifying. The only way to kill the python is by cutting off its head.

How Python Attacks

This spirit wants to keep you from doing what God wants you to do. This is achieved best by the strategy of spiritual apathy. Python wants to quench through suffocation the life and breath of God from your lungs and crush your hopes, faith, visions and dreams. Sometimes this comes through such simple devices as the cares of the world. Financial cares, physical sickness, relationship troubles often produce cares that can constrict the breath of God from a Believer's life and leave them impotent if not dead.

Proverbs 29:18, teaches, "Where there is no vision the people perish..." (become lazy and complacent.) If the devil can crush your hopes, faith, visions and dreams then you will not have the fire you need to "press on to the mark of the high calling of God in Christ Jesus." The devil wants to get your drive, motivation, and fight. This is achieved in many different ways. In one, the devil will whisper in your ears lies, accusations, condemnation, fear and unbelief. The devil always attacks us with words like in the Garden of Eden in Genesis 3, "Has God indeed said?" The devil is always casting doubt and suspicion on God's word, and if we listen long enough, we will also be deceived out of our inheritance, lose heart and give up.

Spirit of Python and Drugs

This spirit is at work in those bound with addictions, particularly smoking or drugs. A spirit of python binds them. At the oracle at Delphi, the priestess would even use laurel leaves, a mildly poisonous plant. Taking in small amounts produced prophetic hallucinations at the place of the oracle. We have seen this spirit at work in those who have received treatment for healing by pursuing the ancient arts of magic or different divinations to alleviate pain.

Hope Deferred

Sometimes Believers who have suffered great trials and tribulations come under the power of crushing grief and the heaviness of disappointment. This can squeeze the life of God, and the power of prophetic promises from the hearts of saints. "Hope deferred" makes the heart sick, and a sense of defeat and impossibility can set in the hearts of the people concerning taking the land.

When the 12 spies were sent in to spy out the land of promise, they returned with a bad report because of the giants in the land. Numbers 13:32, "And they brought up an evil report of the land which they had searched unto the children of Israel, saying, The land, through which we have gone to search, is a land that eateth up the inhabitants thereof; and all the people that we saw in it are men of a great stature."

In Numbers 13:22, "And they ascended by the south, and came unto Hebron; where Ahiman, Sheshai, and Talmai, the children of Anak, were. Their hearts had melted at the giants of Anak in the land."

And they said, "Nevertheless the people are strong that dwell in the land and the cities are walled, and very great: and moreover we saw the children of Anak there," (Numbers 13:28).

They also said, "And there we saw the giants, the sons of Anak, which come of the giants: and we were in our own sight as grasshoppers, and so we were in their sight," (Numbers 13:33).

Even though God had promised in Numbers 13:2, "Send thou men that they may search the land of Canaan, which I give unto the children of Israel," because of their perspective on the situation and the way it looked in the natural, fear and discouragements gripped their heart so that they did not enter into the prophetic promise. This is the way the spirit of Python crushes our faith, vision, hope and dreams. Through discouragement he causes depression, as well as a sense of hopelessness and despair. Depression and the spirit of heaviness bring infirmity, sickness and defeat. It is interesting that the Hebrew translation of the word "Anak" is "to choke as with strangulation using a necklace."

Word Curses

This spirit is often at work around pastor's wives who are battling with fatigue or sickness. Some battle with fibromyalgia or chronic pain and fatigue. Many times it has been the spirit of Python released by those in the church, even other women speaking death words and curses, slander, judgments, and criticism behind her back. Proverbs 18:21 says, "For life and death are in the power of the tongue." After the power of the death words are rebuked, the spirit and affect of Python and fear in the lives of those who had been dominated and even abused by fear and control were set free. The pastor's wives were then released to fulfill God's call.

Remember one of the strategies of this spirit is to

discourage or trod down, which opens the door to depression then infirmity and sickness. Read Proverbs 4:23. "Keep your heart with all diligence, for out of it spring the issues of life." Your heart is the seat of your emotions. What the Bible is saying is that with all diligence we need to protect our mind, will and emotions, because it is the seat for everything that happens in our lives. The devil does not just want to harm your body, but wants to break your spirit through the work of depression. It says in Proverbs 14:30, "A sound or tranquil heart is life to the body."

We need to have a sound heart, and be full of the peace of God that surpasses understanding. Satan wants to disturb the peace in our hearts through anxiety, personal destruction, financial problems, strife in the home, gossip, co-workers, words of condemnation, lies, discouragement and unbelief, crushing our hopes, faith, vision and dreams.

In the chapter called *Time to Civilize,* I purposefully emphasized the motto found on the Branson family crest. I felt like this was a redemptive thread. "Dum Spiro Spero," Latin for "While I breathe, I hope," was an important signpost I believe God had set for us generations ago. Do you still have breath? Then all is not lost. Hope thou in God!

Since the publication of the first edition of this book seven years ago, my husband and I have endured one terrible thing after another including betrayals, tragic and untimely deaths, as well as violent crime. During that time, I was also actively involved in counseling women survivors of child sexual abuse, rape, and incest. All those things along with the cares of the world, and the drought of a move of God combined to press us almost beyond measure. A spirit of heaviness came over us. I almost lost hope.

Each time I neared that sad state, the Lord would send a Word of encouragement to me. It might come from someone during an innocent conversation. It might come through the illumination of the Holy Scripture during my studies. One time it came through a fortune cookie! Nevertheless, the Word would come and raise my chin, lift my face back to the vision of the Glorious King coming in power and might to set the captive free. And I would shoulder my assignment again and move forward.

I live for the day when the apostles of my land and my people produce that Sword of the Spirit, wielded with the arm of faith that will cut off the head of python. I live for the day in which the spring of God will flow throughout our land and set our precious people free. In the meantime, I will hope in God. In the meantime, I will pray, believe and earnestly watch for that victorious day.

CHAPTER SEVENTEEN

REVEALING THE HEADS

"Jezebel strikes viciously at the integrity of the person while the Pharisee spirit of religion has one overriding goal—to set beliefs before relationships."

JEZEBEL SPIRIT

In my dream concerning Python, the first head of this principality that manifested was the head of Jezebel. That was certainly true in my own life. During the same time I was researching and spending hours and hours in prayer and intercession, Jezebel was hard at work attempting to grind me to powder. This demon almost succeeded. What rescued me? The words of affirmation the Lord spoke to me through His Word and the words of affirmation my own husband and friends spoke. During this torturous, confusing, convoluted time, this evil spirit tried diligently to get me to believe things about me that simply were not true.

Perhaps no spirit is more prevalent in the Christian church today than that of the Jezebel. This dangerous, often deadly operator has in its sights the destruction of the church body. Its methods are varied. It knows no gender. It fears no one, but the true prophets of God.

Jezebel is an ambitious, twisted spirit whose power quickly enfolds its victim and injects venom by using manipulation, intimidation, domination and control. We see all aspects of these poisonous attributes at work in I

Kings 21. Unwilling to have her seductive control of Samaria challenged by an uncooperative landholder, Jezebel set in motion a deadly dance. The manipulation began in verse 5. "Why is your spirit so sullen (King Ahab) that you eat no food?" Jezebel feigned loving care. In John Paul Jackson's book, *Unmasking the Jezebel Spirit,* he says the Jezebellite often can be heard saying, "I only say this because I care."

Jezebel turns her destruction to Naboth who must be conquered. At this point, it is not about the vineyard, it is about the power Naboth seems to have because he is the rightful owner. Jezebel *is* the spirit of illegitimacy, the spirit of lawlessness. Jezebel hates true spiritual authority. The land rightfully belonged to Naboth, but Jezebel's ambition burned. Her ambition, and thus inferred loyalty to king and cause, demanded one thing. Naboth must be destroyed.

In verse 13 we see Jezebel's classic method. False witnesses are brought in to discredit Naboth. Jezebel strikes viciously at the integrity of the person. In fact for some ministers and laymen alike who tend the vineyard of the Lord, this blow to the integrity is often so severe and insurmountable it results in the death of one's ministry. Many gifts and callings of God are shipwrecked on the jagged edges of Jezebel's accusations.

Partly, Jezebel succeeds because the scriptural order for resolving disputes is not followed. Paul's letters to Timothy and Titus give wonderful counsel on church order, as well as how to reject divisiveness and resolve disputes.

Jezebel's power operates in conjunction with principalities and powers that torment people (Ephesians 6:12). These demonic powers include spirits of religion, manipulation, control, lust, perversion, and the occult. These spirits often work in concert with a Jezebel spirit to build strongholds in a person's mind. When a Jezebel stronghold is established in a person's mind, I define this as "coming under the influence of a Jezebel spirit." At the moment this occurs, the individual's rational, reasoning process begins to deteriorate. His or her thoughts and actions become distorted (Jackson).

The name Jezebel invokes images of a heavily painted woman whose eyes are bold and whose sexual appetite is voracious. However, many unsuspecting women in the Church are often destroyed when they fall prey to a Jezebel man. The Jezebel spirit works through seduction to affect the course of manipulation, intimidation, domination and control. The pews are littered with the stone-faced, empty remains of women who have been abused by pastoral authority.

On the other hand, the work place and some churches are littered with the shattered remains of ministers whose bodies and souls were seduced and reduced by sexual immorality causing them to vanish from the pulpits.

Several years ago, I dreamed that a missionary friend of mine was in a foreign country riding in a taxi. A woman entered the taxi dressed as a prostitute and seduced him. After praying out the dream, I emailed the contents to my friend in a positive and non-accusatory manner. He responded with humility. Many months later while traveling in another country, he was awakened at 4 a.m. by a phone call to his hotel room. The caller was offering sexual favors. Because his spirit was alerted by the dream and because careful intercession had been done, the missionary vigorously refused and checked out of the hotel the next day. He later admitted a fleeting thought which suggested, "No one would ever know." But inside, the Holy Spirit roared, "But God would know!" He thanked me for sharing the dream. In that case, Jezebel was defeated by a prophetic dream, an obedient messenger and a humble spirit.

This brings us to one of the chief goals of the Jezebel. The Jezebel spirit seeks to destroy the true prophets. As she did in I Kings 19, Jezebel is intent on silencing true prophetic voices. The true prophet is the one who can recognize and reveal Jezebel and survive the malicious backlash that will take place.

The Jezebel spirit can be found operating through or influencing any one of us if we are not careful to soak our hearts in prayers, fasting and humility. Church members deceived by the spirit of pride will always find the Jezebel spirit in others. However, the true Christian will stand before the mirror of the Holy Spirit and earnestly request an evaluation of himself and throw Jezebel down! For further study on this insidious demonic spirit, I highly recommend John Paul Jackson's book.

Pharisee Spirit

The second time the head of Python swung around at me it manifested as the head of a Pharisee. I had to realize the sad truth; there is a little Pharisee in all of us. According to E. Stanley Jones, the Pharisee spirit of religion has one over-riding goal—to set beliefs before relationships. Religious beliefs establish a code of righteousness outside of the relationship with Jesus Christ. That's why Paul concluded, "Our righteousness is as filthy rags." Even a code of goodness cannot compare to a vested relationship. The Pharisee spirit says, "Right is might!" The Lord says, "Right doing is wrong doing when it comes from a wrong heart." Jesus knows hearts may only be truly righted in the presence of the Lord and within the strong bonds of holy fellowship with Him.

The Pharisee spirit is also filled with hypocrisy. Note Jesus' words in Luke 12:1-3: "Beware the leaven of the Pharisees, which is hypocrisy." In other words, the very activating power of Phariseeism is the unsaid, "Do as I say, not as I do." Those held hostage to this spirit live dual lives. Outwardly, they appear to be adorned with righteousness. They always seem to *do right.* In reality, their lives are filled with secret, hidden corruptions. Pharisees tell us to fast, but lie about their own fasting experiences. Pharisees implore others to give, but cannot generously do so themselves. They speak about the "power of the Word," but rarely open the scriptures.

One minister in charge of a deliverance ministry later admitted the reason for her terrible fall was that she cast demons out of people frequently, but rarely prayed or studied the scriptures herself. It wasn't long before the demonic forces had carried her away captive, and she was revealed as a Pharisee.

Paul points a finger at the Pharisee in Romans 2:1, "Therefore you are inexcusable O man, whoever you are who judges, for in whatever you judge another, you condemn yourself; for you who judge practice the same things yourself." Jesus sums up the end of such a one who is ruled by this spirit. "For there is nothing covered that will not be revealed, nor hidden that will not be known. Therefore, whatever you have spoken in the dark will be heard in the light, and what you have spoken in the ear in inner rooms will be proclaimed on the housetops" (Matthew 10:26). Sooner or later, the Pharisee spirit is revealed, without exception. We must challenge ourselves to root this evil out of our own hearts and lives.

Living in truth must be the highest goal. Truth is the very thing Pharisees hate because it is the light which reveals their darkness. That's why this spirit has another powerful insignia. The Pharisee spirit seeks to keep the truth from the people. He loves to keep hidden the truth of God because it creates a sphere of influence for himself. Pharisees love to be the *only* ones who know something. Their modus operendi is "knowledge is power." They do not seek information for transformation. They seek it for demonstration of personal power.

I had an interesting face off with this spirit after the initial printing of this book. Some spiritual leaders decided it must not be provided for intercessors because they personally disagreed with a part of the book. I believe true intercessors are spiritually qualified to read and properly discern the information I have presented. They certainly have the right to agree or disagree, to study, to think, and to discuss the book. The Pharisee spirit, however, will not let that happen lest the power be rested from his hand. No wonder the Pharisees hated Jesus. The Word could not be contained. He walked, talked, worked, and delighted the hearts of the afflicted in spite of that spirit.

This is what I love so much about our Christ; He is so willing to engage us. He is willing to be questioned. When Thomas doubted the veracity of the other disciples' account, Jesus appeared in the room. He didn't come to incinerate Thomas with His fiery gaze. He came gently, softly and tenderly to Thomas and opened his robe. "Here, dear Thomas," He said. "Put your fingers here and your doubts will disappear." Jesus can endure the most stringent questioning. Pharisees on the other hand, cannot abide questioning. They demand absolute obedience and mindless submission. Jesus is not interested in mindless submission. He is a patient teacher who loves to answer the questions of his dear children and readily submits Himself to our examination because He knows we will only find truth in Him.

The Pharisee spirit has another nasty trait. It sucks greedily at the straw of lawlessness. Laws are for everyone else. Those influenced by the Pharisee spirit are above such mundane and restrictive things. However, Watchman Nee once said that we will only walk in as much authority as we are under authority. There is no room for lawlessness in the Kingdom of God. We are all here to serve a Great and Glorious King, not ourselves or our inflated thoughts of our own power and prestige. E. Stanley Jones wrote in *Christ of the Mount*, "The essential difference between Pharisaism and the teaching of Jesus is just here. One was devotion to an idea—the law; the other was a devotion to a Person—the Gospel. The one produced the perfect Pharisee, and the other produced the perfect lover."

A deep, genuine yearning for authenticity in the inward man, an open and honest desire to please the Lord in everything we do, and a reverential fear of God will be our best defense against this soul damning spirit. Again, it will take the unyielding fingers of the Holy Spirit upon our hearts to uncover the Pharisee within us all. Only when we are free of its power can we bring freedom to others.

CHAPTER EIGHTEEN

LEVIATHAN

"In the Siouan (Osage) tongue Wakandagi, as a noun, means a subterranean or water monster, a large horned reptile mentioned in the myths, and still supposed to dwell beneath the bluffs along the Missouri river." J. Owen Dorsey

In the summer of 2003, I saw the dream of Python again. This time I could see the third head which previously was hidden to me. It was a horned serpent. Our pastor had been teaching when he made an observation, "I've traveled to several different countries and have noticed that often the local Catholic Church will link up with the demons resident in that region." Steve and I had also experienced this fact in our missionary journeys to several different countries. In fact, missionary friends of ours have been sorely persecuted in the Philippines by the Catholic Church. In Mexico, missionary apostle David Hogan had a price placed on his head by the Catholic Church. When Pastor made that statement I saw my dream again this time in a day vision.

The Holy Spirit quietly prompted, "What is the name of the Catholic church in Branson?" I easily remembered: Our Lady of the Lake. The Holy Spirit seemed to emphasize the word, lake. I remembered the history of the lake and how it was born from the White River.

Immediately, I remembered a fact that I had overlooked in my study of the Osage: "In the Siouan

(Osage) tongue Wakandagi, as a noun, means a subterranean or water monster, a large horned reptile mentioned in the myths, and still supposed to dwell beneath the bluffs along the Missouri river" (Dorsey).

And from the Cherokee, I remembered: The journey was tortuous in many ways. "Most of the Cherokee were superstitious. They considered rivers, even small creeks to be ways to the underworld; pools were basins of UKTENA, a serpent with supernatural powers" (Ehle).

I was curious about this water serpent. I grabbed my Bible and easily found its name in Job 41 as Leviathan. I searched for understanding regarding this spirit and found on his website Todd Bentley's teaching on the subject.

Bentley's Fall

Since the first publication of this book in 2004, Todd Bentley rose to prominence in America during an outpouring at a Florida healing revival which began April 2, 2008. The move of God was prematurely aborted in August of the same year after reports of Bentley's improper conduct with a female staffer surfaced. Perhaps he fell to the power of Leviathan. Regardless of his inglorious fall, I believe his study on Leviathan is still biblically sound and the revelation of it even more necessary than it was in 2003 when he first published it. I have excerpted some of his teaching here.

Definition of Leviathan

The transliterated Hebrew word for Leviathan (livyathan) means, "twisted," and "coiled." In Job 3:8 in the Revised Version, it denotes the dragon which according to Eastern tradition is an enemy of light.

Job 41:1 refers to the crocodile. In Psalms 104:26 it denotes "any large animal that moves by writhing or wriggling the body, the whale, the monsters of the deep." This word is also used figuratively for a cruel enemy, as some think "the Egyptian host, crushed by the divine power, and cast on the shores of the Red Sea" (Psalms 74:14). As used in Isaiah 27:1, "Leviathan the piercing serpent, even leviathan that crooked serpent."

The following verses offer a fearsome picture of this principality. Job 41:1, "Can you draw Leviathan out with a hook?" Job 41:10, "No one is so fierce that they would dare stir him up." Job 41:26-32, "If one lay at him with the sword, it cannot avail; nor the spear, the dart, nor the pointed shaft. He counteth iron as straw, and brass as rotten wood. The arrow cannot make him flee; sling stones are turned with him to rubble. Clubs are counted as stubble; he laugheth at the rushing of the javelin. His under parts are like sharp potsherds; he spreadeth as it were a threshing wain upon the mire. He maketh the deep to boil like a pot; he maketh the sea like a pot of ointment. He maketh a path to shine after him."

Natural Weapons Have no Power Against Him

It is clear that natural weapons cannot destroy him. Isaiah 27:1 says, "In that day the Lord with his severe sword, great and strong, will punish Leviathan the fleeing serpent, Leviathan the twisted serpent, and he will slay the reptile that is in the sea." It will take the sword of the Lord to overcome this Leviathan; it is more than just a natural, large sea mammal.

Always In the Sea or Rivers

The primary purpose of the spirit is to attack ministries. Psalm 104:25-26 says, “This great and wide sea, in which are innumerable teeming things, living things both small and great. There the ships sail about; there is the Leviathan which you have made to play there.”

When the scripture speaks about the Leviathan, it is always in the sea or in the rivers. The Egyptians both feared and worshiped this creature. They feared him in ancient Greek mythology as the “God of Chaos” and also worshiped him as the great serpent in their rivers responsible for prosperity and good business. The Egyptians believed they had created the rivers just because they learned to use them. This pride was one of Egypt’s greatest sins.

Psalm 104:26 says, “There the ships sail about; there is the Leviathan.” Ships are prophetic of merchants and business. Ships are the ministries of those who are at labor in the “sea of humanity.” This spirit wants to destroy ministries, especially those at labor in the harvest.

It is interesting that not only did Egypt worship this Leviathan, but also that Pharaoh's crown had the emblem of a large serpent with a ruby in it. There is a connection in Ezekiel to this principality and to Egypt and Pharaoh.

Ezekiel 29:3-5 says, “Thus saith the Lord Jehovah; behold, I am against thee, Pharaoh King of Egypt, the great monster that lieth in the midst of his rivers, that hath said, My river is mine own, and I have made it for myself. And I will put hooks in thy jaws, and I will cause the fish of thy rivers to stick unto thy scales; and I will bring thee up out of the midst of thy rivers, with all the fish of thy rivers which stick unto thy scales. And I will cast thee forth into the wilderness, thee and all the fish of thy rivers; thou shalt fall upon the open field; thou shalt not be brought together, nor gathered; I have given thee for food to the beasts of the earth and to the birds of the heavens."

Apparently, this principality worked through Egypt and Pharaoh and even helped to make Egypt what it was.

Leviathan's Seven Heads

Psalms 74:13-14 says, "You broke the heads of the sea serpents in the waters. You broke the heads of Leviathan in pieces. You broke the heads of Leviathan in pieces."

The seven heads or manifestations of Leviathan may be found in Proverbs 6:16-19. "There are six things which Jehovah hateth; Yea, seven which are an abomination unto him; haughty eyes, a lying tongue, and hands that shed innocent blood; a heart that deviseth wicked purposes, feet that are swift in running to mischief, a false witness that uttereth lies and he that soweth discord among brethren."

Like Jezebel, this spirit is anti-Christ and against the anointing on ministries. Leviathan definitely carries the very nature and works of the accuser of the brethren.

How the Spirit of Leviathan Attacks

One of the ways that this spirit will attack is with his tongue. Job 41:1 "Can you draw out Leviathan with a hook, or snare his tongue with a line?" This spirit attacks out of his mouth with lies, gossip, accusation, criticism, faultfinding and slander. Job 41:19 states, "Out of his mouth go burning lights, sparks of fire shoot out."

Leviathan wants you to be destroyed and carried

away with the lies, gossip, slander, and accusations he will bring against you, and if he can he will carry your friends and those who labor with you in the ministry away in the lie and deception. He wants people to believe the lie and accusation against you. Number one, he wants to slander your character and bring reproach on your name.

Wants You to Lash Out Because of Accusations

If the devil cannot trap you in sin, he will accuse you or even make up a lie against you when you are innocent. Proverbs 6:19 says, "A false witness that uttereth lies." This is one of his heads. We need to be sure to respond Biblically to these demonically inspired attacks that even can come from those closest to you. We do not wrestle against flesh and blood. We must respond in a right spirit. We cannot afford to allow Leviathan to operate in us by becoming offended at the lies and accusations, criticisms or judgments spoken about us. To strike back or lash out is what Leviathan wants. It is with his tail in Revelation 12:4, "that he withdrew a third of the angels in heaven. We can only effectively counter attack this spirit by living in truth in every area of our lives."

Miscommunication

Job 42:3 says, "Who is this that hideth counsel without knowledge?" Or in the amplified: "Who is this who darkens or obscures counsel without knowledge?" Or as in another translation; "Who is this who seals up counsel?"

In Job 42:3, the author declares, "Therefore have I uttered that which I understood not. I had heard of thee by the hearing of the ear, but now mine eye seeth thee."

Job is trying to understand what is happening to him. God has this lengthy discussion with Job in chapter 41 and reveals this principality of Leviathan. Job repents in chapter 42 and confesses that counsel and true understanding were kept from him. This spirit wants to get between you and the revelation of God and distort the word of the Lord. The Leviathan spirit will hide the meaning behind what is said and cause there to be miscommunication and misunderstanding. That's how this spirit can sow discord among brethren.

Sons of Pride

Job 41: 34 reads, "He beholds every high thing; He is king over all the children of pride."

This spirit carries an attitude of superiority, haughtiness, boasting and arrogance. He not only works in this kind of environment, but also attacks ministries and individuals with the temptations of pride. This spirit promotes self and self-serving agendas.

Here is a small list of prideful attitudes. Why not ask the Lord to show you any of these in your life?

Condescending Attitudes towards others in the Body: We are to esteem others as higher than ourselves. If we catch ourselves thinking of another as less than ourselves in any way, especially in regards to spiritual gifting, understanding, etc. we must repent quickly.

Independent Attitude: We are to be united in heart as one, although we may all have different functions. If we ever feel we are out there like we just want to do our own thing, maybe we are forgetting the fuller purpose of the

Kingdom, which is to embrace the whole body of Christ.

Self-Glory: Although it is good for one to enjoy the workings, dealings, gifting and blessings that the hand of the Lord brings to us, we must be careful not to think that it is because of our own greatness. All things are given to us as a gift of grace (undeserved, unmerited favor), and all the worship and delight in these blessings must be returned to Him who authored them. We must remember our helpless and humble estate without Him. We can never glory in our own righteousness for to Christ, it is as filthy rags.

Self-Confidence: When we begin to feel a confidence in our own abilities to produce the anointing and the fruit of the Kingdom, we must be alert to the tempter.

Lack of Time in His Presence: Often times this is a sign that one has fallen into pride. It indicates a possibility that we have become self-sufficient and self-ruled and no longer need all that we have and all that we are to flow from His Presence and Counsel. This is dangerous in that it can produce a mindset of "self rule" that subsequently asks God to bless and serve what man has initiated.

Critical and Condemning Attitudes and Thoughts: The heart of a critic or accuser is postured above others. The heart of a Savior is postured in servanthood.

Boasting Over Achievements and Revelation: Often times this is not an outward action but an inward attitude. (Note: this is of the sin nature, not the "boasting in the Lord" of which the Scripture speaks.)

Dishonoring of Authority: We are to esteem and honor

those in authority (even if they are NOT under Holy Spirit control, i.e. David's attitude towards Saul). Attitudes of dishonor toward leaders often indicate pride in the heart.

Desiring to be Served: Jesus did not come to be served, but to serve. This is the posture of humility.

Desire for Reputation: Jesus was a man of no reputation in heart. He emptied Himself. If we have inner desires to be esteemed by others, we need to be watchful. Pride is lurking there.

Desiring to Control Others: One may use a position of authority or gift to fulfill selfish ambition and vision.

The only way we can effectively counter attack this assault is to live in humility. James 4:10 admonishes, "Humble yourselves in the sight of the Lord and he will lift you up." Do you notice it says, "Humble yourselves? This is something we choose to do daily and in every moment when we may feel the attack of Leviathan in pride. Choose to go low!" (Bentley)

The Sower and the Seed

The same year Bentley released his study on Leviathan, in my prayer time I ended up pouring out my frustration to God about why we had not yet seen the move we longed for and felt we had been promised. I heard Him say, "The sower and the seed..." I turned my Bible to Matthew chapter 13. Suddenly verse five was illuminated "Some fell upon stony places where they had not much earth: and forthwith they sprung up because they had no deepness of earth." Into my heart leaped the question, "What is this earth?" I read in verse 20, "But he that received the seed into stony places, the same is he that hears the word and at once with joy receives it; yet he has no root in himself but endures for a while: for when tribulation or persecution arises because of the word, by and by he is offended."

The Holy Spirit unfolded this truth in my heart, "The prophetic destiny of this land has been sown for decades in the hearts of my people, yet because they have refused to die to themselves, their own agendas, ambitions, reputations, and gifting, they easily get offended. They refuse to let tribulations and persecutions kill their flesh. Dead flesh is the earth I need to grow the seed of prophetic promise."

"Choose to go low!" Bentley had counseled. Would to God he had heeded his own words! However, even as I write this I am conscious that except for the grace of God there go I. For that reason, I choose to embrace the knife, let the Lord cut away the horrible and terrible in me and not keep my heart from Him while He does this. I choose to mortify the deeds of the flesh. I choose to humble myself before the Lord because I want so much for my dead flesh to be the earth our Lord needs to bring forth His great and precious promises.

Leviathan's Destruction

After my book was released in 2004, I received sharp criticism from a Catholic leader who was offended by how I said the Lord drew my attention to the subject of Leviathan. He resented me connecting it to the Our Lady of the Lake Parish in Branson. However, two years later, it became apparent that the Lord was speaking to me about much more than I could have realized. An April 20, 2006, a court deposition filed by attorney's for Glenna McKitterick alleged that she was fired from her job with the church after she refused to submit to Father Phillip Bucher's sexual advances. A Boston Globe story from 2002 revealed an affair Bucher had in the early 1980s with a woman. In the late 1990s Bucher purchased a home in Albuquerque, New Mexico with a Springfield woman. In 2006, after the allegations were made public, Bucher quietly retired.

Let me clear up another misconception this gentleman spread concerning me. I have nothing but the greatest respect for Catholic Church members who have been truly born-again and love the Lord Jesus and serve Him only. Those of the Catholic Church or any other church membership for that matter who do not know Jesus Christ as personal Lord and Savior are my concern. They are the subject of my prayers because I want a glorious eternity for them as well as those who have never heard the name of Jesus Christ. I am not "anti-Catholic." I am anti-Leviathan, anti-Satan and anti-sin.

You Broke the Heads of Leviathan

During a community-wide prayer event August 2, 2010, led by long-time area pastors Jay and Kay Scribner the Holy Spirit spoke to me as if commenting on what He had just seen God do. He said, "You broke the heads of Leviathan in pieces, *and* gave him *as* food to the people inhabiting the wilderness." I quickly found the scripture He quoted in Psalm 74:14.

What struck me was that the Holy Spirit illuminated this verse as if it was a new report about current events instead of rehearsing what happened to Egypt when the children of Israel were delivered (because He had done it then too!) It was like the Holy Spirit was currently saying through my spirit, "You just did this!

You broke the heads of Leviathan in pieces, and gave him as food to the people inhabiting the wilderness."

The indication to me was that it was a prophetic "just did," as if by my prophetic prayers and intercession I could declare it, and then go ahead and praise God for doing this just in the same way David was praising Him for doing it in his lifetime, "For God *is* my King from of old, working salvation in the midst of the earth. You divided the sea by your strength; you broke the heads of the sea serpents in the waters (Psalm 74:12-13).

Verses 12 and 13 declare His power to work salvation in the midst of the earth (in the center of our nation/Branson region) and show us the habitation of this principality.

Psalm 104:24-26 identifies the habitation of Leviathan:

> O LORD, how manifold are Your works
> In wisdom You have made them all.
> The earth is full of Your possessions—
> This great and wide sea,
> In which *are* innumerable teeming things,
> Living things both small and great.
> There the ships sail about;
> There *is* that Leviathan
> Which You have made to play there.

This passage begins with glorifying God and recognizing God ultimately even controls Leviathan who plays (makes his plays?) about in the sea where ships are sailing. The picture here is that Leviathan is cavorting about in the water near the harbors, a congested area, where the ships laden with supplies are trying to get into the harbor to unload, but are being hindered by Leviathan. This idea of Leviathan hindering ministries is again borne out in Isaiah 21:1-6 because it takes the destruction of Leviathan to release the fruitfulness of Israel.

> In that day the LORD with His severe sword, great and strong,
> Will punish Leviathan the fleeing serpent,
> Leviathan that twisted serpent;
> And He will slay the reptile that is in the sea.
>
> In that day sing to her, "A vineyard of red wine!
> I, the LORD, keep it,
> I water it every moment;
> Lest any hurt it,
> I keep it night and day.
> Fury is not in Me.
> Who would set briers and thorns
> Against Me in battle?
> I would go through them,
> I would burn them together.
> Or let him take hold of My strength,
> That he may make peace with Me;
> and he shall make peace with Me."
> Those who come He shall cause to take root in Jacob;
> Israel shall blossom and bud,
> And fill the face of the world with fruit.

This indicates that the destruction of Leviathan brings about blossom and bud, and the face of the world filled with fruit. Verse two says that we should sing to

Israel "A vineyard of red wine!" We should prophetically declare vineyards so lush and filled with fruit that it is as if the fruit on the vines are making wine even before they are harvested and processed (won to Jesus and discipled!) We should worshipfully declare the destruction of Leviathan just as David did in Psalm 74. I picture us worshipping God and cheering Him on as He is destroying Leviathan's power in this region.

Remember, the Word of the Lord came to me and said, "You broke the heads of Leviathan into pieces." In Isaiah 27:1, it tells us that "the Lord with His severe sword, great and strong" will do the slaying. We don't have to. In fact, the description Job gives us of Leviathan in Job 41 makes clear that it is impossible for the hand of man to accomplish this. If Leviathan is king over all the children of pride, then humility is the only place of safety during the time God is destroying this evil principality.

So what is our part and why did the Holy Spirit speak this passage to me? The last part of Psalm 74:14 says "and gave him as food to the people inhabiting the wilderness." This indicates the resources, both spiritual and physical, which Leviathan has controlled and kept from the people of God, will be distributed to those "inhabiting the wilderness." If ever we need this we need this now! It will not be distributed to hoarders or those who store up treasures here on earth. It will be distributed for the benefit of those who have been in the wilderness of sin, shame, destruction, torment, slavery and bondages. It will bring life-giving sustenance to those who have been bound in hideous sins.

Ships of ministry full of the Holy Ghost and power are being loosed upon the seas of humanity to work salvation, healing, deliverance, and to teach the Word of God and to make disciples for the Lord Jesus Christ.

I believe I am to sound the trumpet and tell our people that God has already broken the heads of Leviathan. He has broken the heads of Leviathan in my life, in Branson and in my region—this Land of the Osage. Lay hold on the Lord now for the things you have long prayed for. Are there certain souls you have stopped praying for because the discouragement was so great? Pray now and go to them and speak the Good News of Jesus Christ. People will be able to hear what they could not hear before.

Are there dreams and visions you have been given which have fallen by the wayside of discouragement? Lay hold on the Lord for them again. It is time to move into fulfillment. He is near and ready to perform His word.

Prophetic intercessors, faithful prayer warriors, diligent praying men and women of God have pleaded with God in the same way David pleaded in Psalm 74 for the deliverance from Leviathan. God has done it for us. He knows He has done it, the Holy Spirit knows He has done it and the Holy Spirit within us wants to praise our Mighty God for His "wonderful works to the children of men!" I believe He wants us to rejoice with Him that the breakthrough is here. It is time for the performance of the Gospel. It is time to go and preach saying, "The Kingdom of Heaven is here!" Then heal the sick, cleanse the lepers, raise the dead, and cast out devils. Freely we can give because freely we have received.

Israel and Leviathan

There is something else about Leviathan. I will be the first to admit I have no idea what Israel and our region have to do with each other. I am well aware of those ministries headquartered here who also have significant influence in the Holy Land. However, I still do not understand the full scope and significance of what I was recently shown. While working on another writing project, I ran across an article concerning Israel and Leviathan. I was astonished to find that in August, 2010, the same month and year the Holy Spirit said, "You broke the heads of Leviathan..." Houston-based Noble Energy revealed that exploratory drilling off Israel's northern coast confirmed the existence of a major natural gas field. The country's Infrastructure Minister called it "the most important energy news since the founding of the state."

According to the New York Times, "Energy consultants and Israel's top government officials believe this discovery could produce billions in oil and gas revenue for the country and cause Israel to become a gas supplier in the Mediterranean region. The find means that Israel, with a long history of dependence on foreign energy, and hostility and boycotts from many of the biggest energy powers, could find itself in a much more advantageous position in the coming decade."

Can you sing with me "a vineyard of red wine?" Isaiah 21:2

CHAPTER NINETEEN

WISDOM AND WAR

"There was a small city with few men in it and a great king came to it, surrounded it and constructed large siege works against it. But there was found in it a poor wise man and he delivered the city by his wisdom."
Ecclesiastes 9:14-15

In 2004, I had felt for months that I was in a holding pattern concerning the research. The work didn't "feel" complete, yet I was not being given any further direction. One evening I was driving home with my husband when we were both electrified to see the occupants of the vehicle passing us on the highway. It was the high priest and high priestess of the coven traveling together. Although this couple has been well known to us over the years, we could never remember a time when we had seen them traveling together. Our spirits went on "high alert." At a ladies prayer meeting that night, I told fellow intercessors of this strange occurrence. We all agreed to fast through the week that we might be ready for what was about to come. Good thing we did!

That Friday evening, my sister called from a large Branson hotel where she worked. "You have to know this," she said. "We just checked in a group called the Athena Leadership Conference. They are from many different countries and are wearing black garb and pentagram necklaces and rings." God had my sister in the right place at the right time. At various times during the conference, members came to her asking that she make copies of certain hand-outs. When an excited participant came asking her to make copies of the "prophesy" which the goddess Athena had just delivered to the members, my sister quietly accommodated, and made copies for me too.

My research was jump-started in a major way. Athena, or Pallas Athena, is known as the Greek goddess of "wisdom and war" and is one of the most important Olympian deities. According to myth, Hephaestus split Zeus's skull with an ax and out sprang Athena, fully armed. Athena was a deity of diverse functions and attributes. She was a patron of the arts and crafts, especially spinning and weaving. It is important to note for those unfamiliar with the economy of the Branson region, much of our modern tourism industry was founded upon the celebration of pioneer arts and crafts in a themed village called Silver Dollar City. The founders of the theme park are godly people whom I have personally known for years. I supposed this "goddess" was going to be especially called upon to wreck havoc in the business and in the lives of these dear people.

Here are excerpts of Athena's utterances:

> Visualize us in this golden circle holding open a portal. The number of 32 (of us) adding up to 5, to be our number of manifestation and power.......It is with joy in my heart and delight in my soul that I journey here today **to the heartland of this nation *that is destined to change the world.*** It is I, Pallus Athena, visiting you today, riding in the circle of power, as we move together to our destiny....You have gathered today, in this ancient city of old, to carry the symbolism of all Native American

tribes who have ever graced this land. You have come to the centre, like the hub of a wheel, to bring forth the keys and codes that hold the beautiful blessing and teachings that those ancient minds and souls understand....The Sisterhood of the Shields surrounds and protects the vortex that you will open. (According to my research, The Sisterhood of the Shields is "a circle of women who have come together to participate in a process that honors the individual self. Women come together to participate in joint meditations, learning Native American ceremonies and rituals, meeting other women on a similar spiritual path...").

The "prophetic utterance continued, "Melchizedek has directed twelve masters to hold this portal open until the activation is complete at the end of the three days.....I am honored to be placed at the right hand of Mother Mary and I stand next to Sananda, Kuthumi and El Morya as we lead others with the directives from Melchizedek and from metatrons mine. Each of you during this three day gathering shall leave more intelligent and, from this moment in time, your eyes shall be widened, your hearts shall be opened and you will have courage you did not understand residing in your soul.....Hold your vision in the light and let us collectively create this passage for all to journey behind us. For the time has come and our moments are fleeting for when we can now experience our victory and powers....the light radiating from your third eye will only get more intense from this day forward."

The following day another “prophecy” came from Athena:

> It is because of your souls, because of the light and the codes that each of you carry that you have reached a frequency that is connected to the Christ consciousness grid all around. And, each now is able to touch the crossroads on the grid... Open your Third Eye now, and see Them, walk around with Them, as They hold your hands and stand behind you, with Their hands on your shoulders, and on your backs, as They gently guide you....It almost appears as though you no longer need our help, for you have become that which you have claimed you have become...It is I, Pallus Athena, here today with you.....You shall walk now in the days to come, and every place your feet shall trod, you shall leave these sacred (geometric) codes...
>
> We have not marched this way, together in oneness and unity, since the days of Greece, when we collectively took on Poseidon....Those were the days of glory and I want to thank you for bringing me into the consciousness of this world, so that they might see the wisdom, the gifts that I have been given from the Creator, and to fulfill my mission on earth...I am delighted to be the Essence of Mother Mary to bring this through, so that each of you now, can carry that torch and light the way for the world to come...You are distinguished and honored members of the divinity of that which was called the spiritually elite of centuries ago....
>
> What is it, except power to change the course of the world...It is the day you have come back to

> heaven through the earth plane, to become one with the Creator. You must know at this time that the hierarchy was not certain that this would happen. They hoped, and when you had no hope, they held hope; they held the flame within their hearts, that you would walk upon this hallowed ground and that you have reached this point, this sacred moment.

After all that, please note one thing: the words you just read were demonically inspired prophetic utterances so be careful you do not assign them undue value. However, these words do offer important clues to Satan's strategies for our region. Consider these final words through the demon:

"I have not let Apollo come forward. It is not time. We must strategize as we did in Greece, for this balance must be perfect. We must find each other again and celebrate in this moment, before we can expand on this celebration."

Does the name Apollo sounds familiar to you? Yes. It is also called Python. Don't you find it interesting that God would give me the dream about Python years before the demon's own prophetic utterances confirmed its design for our region?

By the second day of the Athena Conference, several area churches and intercessory prayer groups had been informed and were actively praying for our land and our people. John Lindell, pastor of James River Assembly in Ozark, Missouri, offered in his weekly bulletin a careful observation on what was transpiring:

Last night, Debbie and I received an interesting call. The person called to tell us that they had received information that a group of witches and warlocks were meeting at a hotel in Branson. The caller went on to say that the witches and warlocks were concerned over the prominence of Christianity in the area and felt that between midnight and 3 a.m. there would be a strong demonic presence which would empower their endeavors.

The Fall Equinox is one of eight special days in the Wicca calendar, so it shouldn't come as a surprise that witches and warlocks would be meeting. But it was a reminder that even in the Springfield, Missouri area, there is a spiritual battle being waged for the hearts and minds of people.

As I reflected on that call and the spiritual battle we are fighting as Christians, I was reminded of Paul's admonition in Ephesians 6 to put on the full armor of God. A part of that armor is prayer. If we will pray and seek the Lord, He has promised to help us overcome the powers of darkness and we don't have to fear their plans or their power.

The James River Leadership Team had just finished spending the entire day seeking the Lord. As a church we have given ourselves to prayer every Wednesday evening. No amount of money can buy that kind of peace that comes from knowing that because we prayed and sought God's face, the battle is the Lord's... and He will help us stand firm. It's that kind of peace that will allow you to sleep like a baby.

Two months after the Athena Leadership Conference, I thumbed through stacks of research, notes, and clippings when I came across C. Peter Wagner's article, *Territorial Spirits*. I was transfixed by a paragraph I had probably read before, but which now had a whole new meaning:

> Those who exercise a ministry of deliverance (often) discover the names of demons and deal with them personally. As he was ministering to the demonized Gadarene, Jesus asked the spirit's name and it was Legion (Mk. 5:9). If this is done with demons afflicting individuals, it's reasonable to expect that it could also be done with territorial spirits.
>
> I first encountered this kind of spiritual warfare in Argentina with Omar Cabrera. Although he identified territorial spirits and broke their power regularly, his highly intuitive nature did not permit him to analyze for me the principles behind such a ministry.
>
> Another Latin American, Rita Cabezas, has done considerable research on the names of Satan's hierarchy. I will not describe her methods, except to mention that it began with her extensive psychological and deliverance practice and later evolved into her receiving revelatory words of knowledge.
>
> She has discovered that directly under Satan are six worldwide principalities named Damian, Asmodeo, Menguelesh, Arios, Beelzebub, and Nosferasteus. Under each, she reports, are six governors over each nation. For example, those over Costa Rica are Shiebo, Quiebo, Ameneo, Mephistopheles, Nostradamus

and Azazel. Those over the U.S. are Ralphes, Anoritho, Manchester, Apolion, Deviltook, and one unnamed. Each of these governors has been delegated certain areas of evil. For example, the list under Anoritho includes abuse, adultery, drunkenness, fornication, gluttony, greed, homosexuality, lesbianism, lust, prostitution, seduction, sex and vice, while under Apolion we find aggressiveness, death, destruction, discord, dissent, grudges, hatred, homicide, violence and war. Apollyon is mentioned in Revelation 9:11 as the angel of the bottomless pit (Wagner).

I would like to speak a word of caution to those who would attach an unbalanced significance to the demonic utterances of these deceived spirits. We do not receive our revelation from demons; however, I believe when the Lord rips off the cover of their strategies, we should not ignore the information. The Lord used the Athena Leadership Conference to reveal that a high level strategy from Satan exists against our region. We cannot ignore that fact. Jesus urged us to be wise as serpents and harmless as doves. Athena is supposedly the goddess (demon) of wisdom and war. The truth is Jesus is wisdom and by Him we shall win this war.

CHAPTER TWENTY

BY HIS WISDOM

"On the plains of hesitation lay the blackened bones of countless millions who on the verge of victory sat down to rest and while resting, died." General George S. Patton

Apollo, Apollyon, Python, or the spirit of divination, are one and the same demon—and according to Cabezas, this principality is one of the six governors over our nation. The prophets who came and prophesied and who were completely unknown to each other confirmed that it is so. These confirmations along with my dream make me feel confident I am on the right track since the scripture says, "In the mouth of two or three witnesses, let every word be established."

I have long pondered the significance of what I believe I have discovered. When I began my research and prayer seven years earlier, all I was really looking for was the answer to what had opposed me and what I could do about it. I wanted to know how this power came to be, what its root systems were, and where the untruths were in me that gave power to this enemy. For that reason, I had begun my research focused on our first people.

Seven years later, the demon channeled at the Athena conference caused me to remember the beginning of my research when it said, "You have gathered today, in this ancient city of old, to carry the symbolism of all

Native American tribes who have ever graced this land. You have come to the centre, like the hub of a wheel, to bring forth the keys and codes that hold the beautiful blessing and teachings that those ancient minds and souls understand."

The major themes that stand out to me in my research is: superstition (including all forms of religious superstitions), secret societies (including all forms of pharisaic behaviors that attempt to hide knowledge from the people), lawlessness and revenge (including all forms of lawless greed), and racial supremacy (including all forms of racial divisions). I believe these are all abhorrent to the God of heaven and earth who made us all to be one with Him through His Son Jesus Christ.

I think it is also important to note that the demon that was channeled at the Athena Conference was merely noting what people of God have known for years and years. This region is:

"...the heartland of this nation that is destined to change the world."

That line sounds very close to this section of the 1998 prophecy from Reverend Tim Snider which I included in the first chapter of this book:

> For God is calling into the middle of this country an area and a place where God is going to cause to flow forth into this country and into this world a people that are not ashamed of the gospel, a people that are not fighting with one another, but a people that are linked together and will say, "God is God. We are not here to represent ourselves, but we are here to represent God, the Lord God Jehovah.

I will not pretend I can even begin to understand all of what that means. I do, however, believe this amazing gathering of Christians that has been taking place in this region is part of a divine design that is much bigger than any single one of us.

What could change the world? I imagine it is the manifestation of the glory of God in the sons of man. I imagine it as a great wave of glory revealed through God's Beloved Bride that brings innumerable healings, miracles, signs and wonders, life-changing salvations, overnight restorations, the renewing of the mind, and the miraculous healing of wounded souls. I imagine it is the Church so powerfully on fire and in passionate love with their Lord that the whole world will be turned upside down one more time before His long-awaited return. I imagine that it will be the glorious Church without spot or wrinkle, washed, purified and made ready. I imagine it as a host of men and women, boys and girls who can see the light of God in each other's eyes before they ever ask about denominational affiliation.

Is my imagination too big? More likely, too little. To ever see such a breathtaking thing we must be absolutely sure "Satan hath nothing in me..." We must be completely sure we have repented for personal sins and the sins of our people so that "no weapon formed against us can prosper." Finally, we must "hold fast to the profession of our faith without wavering." We must get a death grip on the great and precious promises God has made for our land and people, and we must fight until the victorious conclusion so that this great harvest of souls can begin.

"Cry aloud, spare not, lift up thy voice like a trumpet, and show my people their transgression and the house of Jacob their sins" (Isaiah 58:1).

"If my people which are called by my name, shall humble themselves and pray and seek my face, and turn from their wicked ways; then will I hear from heaven and will forgive their sin and will heal their land" (II Chronicles 7:14).

"And even if our gospel is veiled, it is veiled to those who are perishing, in whose case the god of this world has blinded the minds of the unbelieving that they might not see, less the light of the glorious gospel of Christ, who is the image of God, should shine in them." (II Corinthians 4:3-4).

"For we wrestle not against flesh and blood, but against principalities, powers, against rulers of the darkness of this world, against spiritual wickedness in high places" (Ephesians 6:12).

Where Do We Go From Here?

The hope I carry prayerfully within me is that Church leadership and praying members of our region will apply something of what this research offers and humbly repent, prayerfully intercede, and powerfully oppose. Submit to God. Resist the devil.

I believe "what God reveals He wants to heal." This research is not intended to divide Christian denominations by revealing mistakes of the past. We each have plenty for which to repent, no matter what church considers you a member. Furthermore, it is not my intent to exonerate any group of Believers over another. Instead, it is my hope that as a people, we will accept the burden of our guilt in the same way Ezra accepted the guilt of his people.

I pray that we will repent and ask God to cleanse us from our historical sins which if left to grow, offer rich root systems for our sins of today. I pray that as we repent God will prevent the cycle of sins from staining our future generations.

Let me ask you a question. Do you believe demons are assigned to people in order to manifest Satan's plans and purposes through them? Where do these demons go when that person through whom they are working dies? The demons are not buried with the carcass of that human machinery they employed. Those particular demons do not abandon their historical assignments. What do you suppose they do? I imagine they cast about and discover another human machine through which they can accomplish their evil purposes. We must deny them access to lives by bringing the light of the Gospel to people so they refuse demonic powers access and opportunity. Deception begets deception. It can do no other thing. Only truth can beget the truth needed to set lives free from being instruments of demonic destruction.

I hope that our people will collectively refuse this enemy any further authority in our region; that we will "wrestle against this principality" and all the powers associated with him. I pray that we will not move independently or presumptuously, but carefully and war-like with a well-defined strategy for victory. I pray that we move humbly and reverently before our God so that He will release the armies of Heaven to come to our aid.

Finally, I pray that we ready ourselves for the deluge of souls that will assuredly pour into God's Kingdom when the enemy of the region has been defeated. May we become "new, sharp threshing instruments with teeth" (Isaiah 41:15). May we become as a land and people all that we were meant to become. May we destroy every division and work together with respect for each other and the Harvest! And above all, may we have unquenchable charity for each other, for the lost sinners and for Our Lord.

We must be famous for the great love and fellowship in Christ we have for our brothers and sisters, no matter their denominational affiliation. We must be known for our tender care and compassionate ministry to the lost and dying sinners. We must be known for the glory of God's love so saturating our very beings that all those around us want to know our Majestic King.

We must be people of passion who believe that lives depend on what we do. Proverbs 24:11-12 declares, "Deliver those who are drawn toward death, and hold back those stumbling to the slaughter. If you say, 'Surely we did not know this,' does not He who weighs the hearts consider it? He who keeps your soul, does He not know it? And will He not render to each man according to his deeds?"

Many of us have been in this battle for a long time. I know from personal experience it is easy to grow weary in the fight. Cares of life, personal disappointments, and devilish assaults can combine to reduce us to a rag-tag bunch. But I am sending out a call to arms today. Soldiers of the Living God have you come to fail? Have you fought this long and this hard for nothing? Are not the King of Glory and His plans worth the price? Take up arms again! Take up the truth of God through His written Word! Take up the personal prophecy you were given that brought you here!

General George S. Patton once wrote, "On the plains of hesitation lay the blackened bones of countless millions who on the verge of victory sat down to rest and while resting, died." I am more convinced than ever that the Third Great Awakening is even at the door. I am more convinced than ever that angelic hosts are preparing for that moment when the sword of the spirit takes off the head of that serpent. I am more convinced than ever that we are moments away from the time the cup of intercession is full, and the mercy of God will be poured out across our land.

Will you be convinced with me? Will you cleanse your hands and hearts? Will you pray and intercede with me? Why are you here? Why have you come to this place?

Who knows but what you have come to this place for such a time as this?

WORKS CITED

Chapter One

Prophetic message spontaneously delivered by Pastor Tim Snider - October 12, 1997 Oak Ridge Full Gospel Church, (now Healing River Worship Center) Branson, MO.

Prophetic message spontaneously delivered by Jeanne Wilkerson, April 1982, Harrison, AR.

Prophetic message spontaneously delivered by Pastor Guy Johnston, February 22, 1995, Life Christian Center, Branson, Missouri

Prophetic message spontaneously delivered by Pastor Clyde J. Avery, January 31, 1999, Peoples' Church Rainbow Tabernacle, Roaring Creek, Virginia

Prophetic message spontaneously delivered by Pastor Tim Snider, October 29, 1998, Oakridge Full Gospel Church, (now Healing River Worship Center), Branson, MO.

Parnell, Todd. *The Branson We Know, a Family Narrative*, self-published, Springfield: 2001.

Chapter Two

Rafferty, Milton D., Ph. D. *Rude Pursuits and Rugged Peaks: Schoolcraft's 1818-1819 Ozark Journal*. Fayetteville: University of Arkansas Press, 1996.

Bennett, W. J., Jr. and Jeffrey A. Blakely. Archeological and Historical Investigations Old Forsyth Site (23TA41) Taney County, Missouri, ARCHEOLOGICAL ASSESSMENTS, INC. NASHVILLE: December, 1987.

Spelling, T.C. *Taney Enterprise*, Forsyth, Missouri, March 1, 1883, Volume 2

Hoenshel, E.J. and L.S. Hoenshel, *Stories of the Pioneers.* Branson: 1915.

Wagner, C. Peter, *Territorial Spirits*, 1989.

Chapter Three

Mahnkey, Mary Elizabeth Prather. Ozark Lyrics, Branson: July 1, 1934.

Rafferty, Milton D., Ph. D. *Rude Pursuits and Rugged Peaks: Schoolcraft's 1818-1819 Ozark Journal*. Fayetteville: University of Arkansas Press, 1996.

Wright, Harold Bell. *The Shepherd of the Hills.* New York: A.L. Burt Company, 1907.

Lisby, Gaye. "The River Runs Through It." *Branson Living Magazine* October/November 1996.

Chapter Four

Ingenthron, Elmo. *Indians of the Ozarks Plateau.* Point Lookout: The School of the Ozarks Press, 1970.

Dorsey, J. Owen. *Reports of the Bureau of Ethnology*: Third annual report of the Bureau of Ethnology to the Secretary of the Smithsonian Institution, 1881-82.

Mathews, John Joseph. *The Osages: Children of the Middle Waters.* University of Oklahoma Press, 1961.

Bailey, Garrick. *The Osage and the Invisible World: from the works of Francis La Flesche*. University of Oklahoma Press, 1995

Chapter Five

Ehle, John. *Trail of Tears.* New York: Anchor Books, 1988.

Rafferty, Milton D., Ph. D. *Rude Pursuits and Rugged Peaks: Schoolcraft's 1818-1819 Ozark Journal*. Fayetteville: University of Arkansas Press, 1996.

Stacey Family History, unpublished

Bennett, W. J., Jr. and Jeffrey A. Blakely. Archeological and Historical Investigations Old Forsyth Site (23TA41) Taney County, Missouri, ARCHEOLOGICAL ASSESSMENTS, INC. NASHVILLE: December, 1987.

Spelling, T.C. *Taney Enterprise*, Forsyth, Missouri, 1883.

Chapter Six

DeArmond, Fred. *Missouri's Tennessee Heritage.* 1970.

DeArmond, Fred. "Scotch-Irish Heritage." *White River Valley Historical Quarterly*, Vol. 4, NO. 4, Summer 1971.

Littleton, C. Scott, Ph.D. *Mythology and Folklore*. 1993.

The Druid Path. http://druidry.org/obod/druid-path/index.shtml

Massey, Ellen Gray. Editor, *Bittersweet Country.* New York: Anchor Books, 1978.

Chapter Seven

Randolph, Vance. *Ozark Superstitions.* New York:Vanguard Press, 1946

Bailey, Garrick. *The Osage and the Invisible World: from the works of Francis La Flesche*. University of Oklahoma Press, 1995

Ingenthron, Elmo. *Indians of the Ozarks Plateau.* Point Lookout: The School of the Ozarks Press, 1970.

Vann, David. http://cherokeeblood.blogspot.com

Rafferty, Milton D., Ph. D. *Rude Pursuits and Rugged Peaks: Schoolcraft's 1818-1819 Ozark Journal*. Fayetteville: University of Arkansas Press, 1996.

Mooney, James. "Myths of the Cherokee." *19th Annual Report, Bureau of American Ethnology*, 1900.

Chapter Eight

Ingenthron, Elmo and Mary Hartman. *Borderland Rebellion.* Gretna: Pelican Publishing Company, 1988.

Sechler, Earl T. *Our Religious Heritage: Church History of the Ozarks, 1806-1906* Springfield: Westport Press, 1961.

Hoenshel, E.J. and L.S. Hoenshel, *Stories of the Pioneers.* Branson: 1915.

Excerpted from the unpublished diary of Lt. C.W. Huff, stationed with the Union troops, Forsyth, MO.

Monks, Col. William, *"Stories of the War Years."* West Plains: West Plains Journal Company, 1907

Chapter Nine

Mackey, Albert G. *Encyclopedia of Freemasonry,* 1917

Pike, Albert. *Morals and Dogma,* published by the Supreme Council of the Thirty Third Degree for the Southern Jurisdiction of the United States Charleston, 1871.

Mahnkey, Douglas. *Bright Glowed My Hills*. Point Lookout: The School of the Ozarks Press, 1968.

Chapter Ten

Sermon by Brigham Young, Journal of Discourses, Vol. 4, pages 53-54); also published in the Mormon Church's Deseret News, 1856, page 235)

Online: *What shocked you the most? (for those who were Mormons),* December 24, 2007.

Chapter eleven

Ingenthron, Elmo and Mary Hartman. *Borderland Rebellion.* Gretna: Pelican Publishing Company, 1988.

Editorial, *Springfield Republican.* 1886.

Spellings, T.C., Publisher. *Taney Enterprise* , Thursday, March 1, 1883.

Chapter Twelve

Hodges, Pearl, *"Thomas Jefferson Berry."* White River Valley Historical Quarterly, Winter, 1968-69.

Chapter Thirteen

Unknown author, *The Forgotten Man,* self-published, 1888.

Brittain, Almeda, *Pioneer Preacher of the Ozarks*

Yeoman, William Pope. *The General Baptist History.* Stephens, 1899.

Bonnie Youngblood, telephone interview. 1998

Chapter Fourteen

Hoenshel, E.J. and L.S. Hoenshel, *Stories of the Pioneers.* Branson: 1915.

Ingenthron, Elmo and Mary Hartman. *Borderland Rebellion.* Gretna: Pelican Publishing Company, 1988.

Hartman, Viola. *The Ghost of Gobbler's Knob and Other Tales of the Hill Country*. Branson: Mountain Country Marketing, 1982.

Chapter Fifteen

Dake, Finnis Jennings. *Dake Annotated Reference Bible.* Lawrenceville, Georgia: Dake Bible Sales, Inc. 1963.

Chapter Seventeen

Jackson, John Paul. *Unmasking the Jezebel Spirit,* North Sutton, NH: Streams Publications, 2002.

Jones, E. Stanley. *Victorious Living.* New York: The Abiingdon Press, 1936.

Chapter Eighteen

Dorsey, J. Owen. *Reports of the Bureau of Ethnology*: Third annual report of the Bureau of Ethnology to the Secretary of the Smithsonian Institution, 1881-82.

Ehle, John. *Trail of Tears.* New York: Anchor Books, 1988.

Bronner, Ethan, *"Gas Field Confirmed Off Coast of Israel."* The New York Times, December 30, 2010

Chapter Nineteen

Wagner, C. Peter, *Territorial Spirits*, 1989.

Look for These

Other Books By
Gaye Newman Lisby

And Sapphire Throne, Inc.

The Spiritual History of the Land of the Osage and Branson (First Edition)

God Within Us-Experiencing the Holy Spirit

Victorious Living-Becoming a Comeback Kid in a Knock-Down World, by Tim Snider with Gaye Lisby

My Name Is God
A Loving Father Introduces Himself to His Children
(2011 Fall Release Date)

Follow Gaye's blog:
www.sapphirethrone.blogspot.com

Gaye Lisby is available for speaking engagements, conferences and retreats. Please contact:
Sapphire Throne, Inc. 190 Mary Lane,
Kirbyville, MO 65679 sglisby@juno.com
or find Gaye on Facebook!

Made in the USA
Monee, IL
10 February 2024

53224902R00152